THE INDOMITABLE PROPHET

The Indomitable Prophet

A Biographical Commentary on Jeremiah:
The Man, the Time, the Book, the Tasks

R. E. O. White

WILLIAM B. EERDMANS PUBLISHING COMPANY
GRAND RAPIDS, MICHIGAN

Copyright © 1992 by William B. Eerdmans Publishing Co.
255 Jefferson Ave. S.E., Grand Rapids, Mich. 49503
All rights reserved

Printed in the United States of America

Library of Congress Cataloging-in-Publication Data

White, R.E.O. (Reginald Ernest Oscar), 1914–
The indomitable prophet: a biographical commentary on Jeremiah:
the man, the time, the book, the tasks / R.E.O. White.
p.   cm.
Includes indexes.
ISBN 0-8028-0529-9
1. Bible. O.T. Jeremiah — Criticism, interpretation, etc.
2. Jeremiah (Biblical prophet).   I. Title.
BS1525.2.W47   1991
224'.206 — dc20   91-41818
                                   CIP

Contents

v

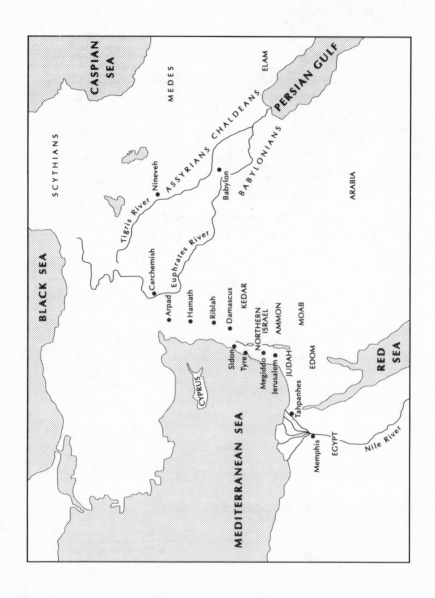

JEREMIAH'S WORLD

Outline of Period

Throughout this text, all dates are B.C. Some uncertainty about the dates is due in part to the fact that Hebrew chroniclers sometimes reckoned years "exclusively" (counting 510 B.C. to 500 B.C. as *ten* years), and sometimes reckoned them "inclusively" (counting 510 B.C. to 500 B.C. as *eleven* years). However, the difference is not important for understanding the book of Jeremiah.

The following are approximate dates of the events listed:

722	Northern Israel overrun, exiled; one of the later years of *Hosea*'s ministry
715-687	*Hezekiah* king of Judah
687-642	*Manasseh* king; *Zephaniah* ministers during later years
642-640	*Amon* king
650 to 645	*Jeremiah* born
648	Josiah born
640-609	*Josiah* king

626   Jeremiah called to prophesy; Scythians (in 626 or 620) threaten invasion

622 or 621   Josiah's reform begins

609 or 608   Battle of Megiddo; Josiah is killed. *Jehoahaz* king for three months; removed by Egypt

608-597   *Jehoiakim* king

605   Battle of Carchemish

604   Nebuchadrezzar rules Babylon (until 561)

597   *Jehoiachin* king for three months; removed along with leaders to Babylon

597-586   *Zedekiah* king

586   Jerusalem destroyed, and king and "best of the people" removed to Babylon; Gedaliah appointed governor

586 or 582   Gedaliah assassinated; Jewish peasants, with Jeremiah, removed to Egypt, where Jeremiah dies

1

A Truly Remarkable Man

The prophet Jeremiah was indeed, from several points of view, a most remarkable man. His gifts of eloquent persuasion and forceful argument, his involvement in public affairs, and his intense patriotism could have made him a great statesman. Had he brought his sharpness and integrity of mind to bear upon abstract questions in the Greek fashion, he would have ranked as a philosopher. With his immense courage and tenacity of purpose, his grasp of world movements and the consequences of great battles, he might even have become one of the ancient world's great soldiers.

Add to all this Jeremiah's varied poetry, his talent for dramatic expression of his meaning, and his wide-ranging knowledge, and it becomes obvious that he was a man of considerable stature and manifold potential. But he gave his life wholly to the service of God among his own people, and — scandalously — he is best known as "the weeping prophet." His very name is grossly distorted and misused as a derogatory epithet for complaining weakness, pessimism, and self-pity: a "jeremiad."

1

That exposes an inexcusable failure to appreciate the only vital personality still influencing the world from that half-century of cosmic upheaval into which Jeremiah was born. It exposes also an equally inexcusable (though centuries old) assumption that Jeremiah wrote that almost unrelieved dirge over Judah's tragic ruin which we know as the book of Lamentations. Unfortunately, ability and faithfulness in the sphere of religion are rarely paths to lasting fame. Yet after twenty-six centuries Jeremiah remains one of the spiritual leaders of humankind.

For two original insights of permanent importance (besides much else), Jeremiah has been described by one commentator as "one of the world's supreme discoverers in the greatest of all realms." These are (1) that the *basis* of religious life is a voluntary, binding covenant with God, in which God freely offers the terms, and the individual as freely accepts, and finds his or her highest welfare in so doing; and (2) that the *heart* of all genuinely religious experience is an intimate, individual (yet also shared) fellowship with God, in which divine revelation and love are met by prayer, confession, and trust. Tentative foregleams of these insights may be found, and numerous later developments of them; their clearest assertion, together, begins with Jeremiah.

Background

Jeremiah was born about 650/645 B.C., in the closing years of the long reign of Manasseh over the small, remote hill-state of Judah in southern Palestine. At that time Judah was a tributary province, and Manasseh a vassal king, of the great empire of Assyria. Jeremiah's home was at Anathoth, a village a few miles north of Jerusalem.

Anathoth was the site of an ancient shrine dedicated to Anath, the North Syrian goddess of war, revered in Israel as "the queen of heaven," and later, in Elephantiné (in Egypt), alongside Jehovah as his consort Anath-yahu. It was to Anathoth that Solomon had banished David's priest Abiathar, a descendant of Eli, high priest at Shiloh. Here at Anathoth a priestly colony remained, rivaling the "Zadokite" priesthood at Jerusalem.

Anathoth's priests served its famous hill-shrine and prospered under Manasseh. Their worship combined older Canaanite rites with those associated with Abraham and Moses. The traditional faith of the patriarchs was thus mingled with ideas from ancient native idolatry, and with acknowledgment of the Canaanite fertility gods or spirits, the "Baals." Born of a Levite family, himself a priest and maintained by the priests' due "portion" (37:12), Jeremiah grew up in this confusing syncretist atmosphere.

But barely ten miles north of Anathoth lay the border of the former northern kingdom of Israel, which only seventy-five years before had been overrun by Assyrian forces and its people transported to Mesopotamia. Jeremiah would be taught that this was a divine punishment for Israel's apostasy. Moreover, within reach (if not actually within sight) of Jeremiah's home was the ruin of Shiloh, where Eli's sons had been rejected from the priesthood, where Samuel the prophet and king-maker had heard God's call, and where eventually fire had utterly destroyed God's shrine. This too, Jeremiah would be told, was punishment for disloyalty to the God of Abraham, Isaac, and Jacob.

All these boyhood stories, impressions, and images lingered in Jeremiah's mind; in later years they would disturb his conscience, shape his thought, and color his language.

Knowledge

Israel's priests were charged with the instruction of the people, and Jeremiah's "professional" training explains his thorough knowledge of his nation's history, religion, and literature. His early preaching and poetry, especially 3:6-18, reveal acquaintance with the message of the northern prophet, Hosea, and other echoes of earlier writings are equally plain, in particular those of Amos and of Isaiah of Jerusalem.

But whence came Jeremiah's extensive knowledge of the personalities, policies, geography, and religions of the Middle East? He knew so much, not only of former northern Israel ("Samaria" or "Ephraim") and Lebanon, but of Damascus, Tyre, and Sidon, and further north, even to Hamath; of the Scythians invading Asia Minor; of the river Euphrates, Babylon, Chaldea, Media, and Elam at the head of the Persian Gulf; of Egypt and Ethiopia to the far south; of Philistia and Cyprus to the west; and of Gilead and distant Kedar and Hazor on the edge of the eastern wilderness, with Edom, Moab, Ammon, and the Arab tribes.

Nor were these mere names to Jeremiah. He listed their many cities, revealing knowledge of their position. He knew the rocky heights of Edom, the deep glens of Moab, the rising and falling of the Nile, the massive walls and wide moats of Babylon. He knew the names of foreign kings, the outlandish titles of foreign officers of state. He knew of the salt lands beyond the Dead Sea, the winds of the Euphrates delta, the dark skins of the Ethiopians — and all without a map.

Jeremiah knew the varying customs and religions of different lands, the names of many gods and goddesses, the feasts observed, the sacrifices required, the rituals followed, the trimming of hair and beards and other strange rites practiced. The book of Jeremiah provides a well-informed handbook of comparative religion for the Near East of his time. Trade, travel, military expeditions, and the civil organization of a great empire all served to foster the flow of information and the international "commerce of thought." Jeremiah evidently took great advantage of his opportunities.

Nearer home, and with profit to his poetry, Jeremiah

watched or heard of metal refiners, shepherds, archers, horse-men, potters, reapers, fowlers, fishers, hunters, craftsmen, smiths, woodsmen, Arabs waylaying travelers in the deserts, and thieves. He knew that debtors' gratitude turns easily to hatred of their creditors; he knew the ways of grape gatherers and wine makers; he understood the unscrupulous use that scribes could make of their skill.

Nature, too, taught Jeremiah much. He observed with care the returning stork "who knows her times," turtledoves, swallows, cranes, the "deaf" uncharmable adders, the lairs of jackals, the speckled bird ostracized by its mates. He saw wild asses panting for water, gadflies tormenting cattle, "bristling" locusts, "slithering" serpents, "restive" young camels in heat "interlacing their tracks," and the eagle's enormous wing-span high above her lofty nest.

Jeremiah shared the popular belief that the partridge gathers a brood it did not hatch. He seems to have watched a forest lion breaking cover to scatter a panic-stricken flock across the hillside. He described the desert wolf, the "watchful" leopard, the owl (NIV; "ostrich," RSV) inhabiting ruins with hyenas. All this, of course, without any of the aids to accumulated knowledge that we now take for granted. And he responded to what he saw. He was deeply impressed by the orderliness of the universe, the "covenant" of day and night, the fixed order of the stars' movements, the limits set for the sea, the immeasurable immensity of the heavens, and the immovable foundations of the earth. He was a remarkably well-informed man.

Jeremiah's Call

1:4-12 Clearly, all nature spoke to Jeremiah "rememberable things." But especially the first tree to bud at Anathoth, heralding another springtime, the early-flowering almond. It was by that "sign," in the spring of 626 B.C., when Jeremiah was between twenty and twenty-three years of age, that Jeremiah the priest was called of God to be a "prophet."

Immediately when the word is used it demands definition. Certainly Old Testament prophets sometimes predicted events, but *never* by the stars, by crystal balls, or by the entrails of animals. They observed and interpreted the trends of their time, foresaw and described the probable outcome of present policies and behavior. Samuel predicted the end of Saul's reign because Saul had forfeited God's favor. Jeremiah predicted Judah's fall and exile because fifty years of decadence had left her helpless before the westward sweep of Babylon.

But *prediction was not the prophet's main function,* and Jeremiah was not very good at it. Some prophets were counselors to kings, either maintained by them to support royal policies or independent advisers and critics of the kings' intentions. Some taught religion at countryside shrines, either professionally or as voluntary and independent preachers. Some performed miracles. All commented upon public affairs and private behavior in the name of God, conscience, and common sense.

As preachers, the prophets used all the skills of oratory, poetry, and argument at their command. Since their hearers were mainly nonliterate, poetry was more attractive to hear and more easily remembered. (Jeremiah is among the Old Testament's finest poets.) Another device for aiding memory was the linking of meaning with names of places and persons, forming serious "puns" by which any recurrence of the name would immediately recall the message attached to it (see 1:11-12; 19:1–20:6; 23:2; 48:21).

Some prophets were also actors; by dramatic actions their announcements, warnings, and counsel were written upon the memory, provoked discussion, and sometimes were believed to set in motion the fulfillment of what was spoken. So Jeremiah first wore, then buried, a new waistcloth (13:1-11); publicly

smashed an earthen flask (19:1-11); walked Jerusalem's streets
with a yoke bound upon his shoulders (chaps. 27–28); buried
paving stones (43:8-10); bought a field (chap. 32); instructed
that a scroll be sunk in the Euphrates (? 51:59-64); invited
teetotaling Rechabites to a wine-tasting (chap. 35); and, perhaps partly with the same symbolic intent, remained unmarried
(16:1-4). Jeremiah was a most versatile publicist.

Genuine prophets believed that God upheld the right and
kept his promises. Given moral insight, alert consciences, independent minds, great courage, and in many cases the poet's
gift for seeing things clearly and saying them unforgettably,
the prophets spoke God's mind to their own time, and warned
— or promised — how things would turn out. Such was
Jeremiah called to do.

In earlier days, such prophets had been called "seers"
(1 Sam. 9:5-9) because they perceived more in the world about
them than other people could see. Perhaps one would need
something of this God-given "second sight" to discern exactly
what Jeremiah saw in the early-blossoming almond tree that
arrested his attention. It had something to do with a pun upon
the tree's Hebrew name, which closely resembled the word for
"watching." It brought to Jeremiah's mind, in a very evil time,
the assurance that despite everything God was still watching
over his pledged word to Judah and would perform it. There
was hope still, after the dark winter of Manasseh's reign, of
another spiritual springtime for God's people.

With that stimulating insight came God's call: "Before I
formed you in the womb I knew you, and before you were born
I consecrated you; I appointed you a prophet to the nations"
(1:5). Formed for it, born to it, consecrated for it, appointed,
and now called: that cumulative sense of destiny never wholly
left Jeremiah thereafter — nor let him alone.

Yet Jeremiah's immediate reaction was to object to the
call on the grounds of his youth and his inarticulateness. Like

Moses, Gideon, David, and Isaiah of Jerusalem, the young Jeremiah flinched at God's call to service. He was wholly reluctant to respond, not because he was unwilling but because he was unsure of his ability. Perhaps, too, he saw neither romance nor glory in the prospect of becoming a prophet, as he remembered the responsibility shouldered by and the harsh reception experienced by men like Hosea, Amos, and Isaiah.

This reluctance never wholly left Jeremiah, either. To the end of his long ministry it wrestled with the sense of duty imposed by his unsought destiny, causing him intense discomfort. The time would come when Jeremiah would protest vigorously against the vocation to which he had been born and appointed: "O that I had in the desert a wayfarers' lodging place, that I might leave my people and go away from them!" (9:2); "Be not a terror to me" (17:17); "O Lord, thou hast deceived me. . . . If I say, 'I will not mention him, or speak any more in his name,' there is in my heart as it were a burning fire" (20:7, 9). For Jeremiah there could be no evading historical facts or moral forces; he must speak the harsh, unwelcome truth. But he found it as bitter to utter as to hear.

God's initial answer to his reluctant young prophet was firm and reassuring: "Do not say, 'I am only a youth'; for to all to whom I send you you shall go. . . . Be not afraid of them, for I am with you to deliver you. . . . Behold, I have put my words in your mouth. See, I have set you this day over nations and over kingdoms, to pluck up and to break down, to destroy and to overthrow, to build and to plant" (1:7-10). If the promise was encouraging, the job description was utterly daunting.

Adversity

Jeremiah's nervous, retiring temperament, which loved simple human things but above all *peace;* his inner insecurity and outward lack of confidence; his inescapable sense of duty — in later years these were the sources of Jeremiah's intense suffering. He agonized, as any clear-eyed realist must in desperate situations, but with a poet's added sensitiveness, a patriot's grief, and almost a woman's tenderness, for the wives and children soon to be kidnapped, exiled, or butchered by invading enemies. For all that, when he was criticized, treated with contempt, or threatened, Jeremiah could show himself to be a man of fiery spirit, as sensitive men often do.

Additional grounds for young Jeremiah's apprehension included the dreadful moral and religious climate of the age. His passionate love for his land and his people made the message he had to bring — "terror on every side" (6:25; 20:3, 10; 46:5; 49:29) — a burden to him. To his contemporaries it seemed plain sedition and betrayal. His warning that Jerusalem would surely be destroyed sounded like blasphemy, given the earlier promise of Isaiah of Jerusalem that the city would be inviolate, and the assurance of Hosea that God's love for Israel was unchanging.

Jeremiah found that the appeal to recorded words of God, in past generations and in different circumstances, was always selective. Where others found comforting promises, he discovered only solemn warnings. Besides, state-supported "prophets" abounded, pledged to affirm divine authority for official policies; amid so many voices claiming to speak in God's name, it was difficult, even for earnest hearts, to discern God's truth. On at least one occasion, Jeremiah seems to have doubted his own message.

Again, in attacking the religious practices of his day, Jeremiah was embarrassed by his own status as a priest, because he was publicly opposing his own class and kinsmen. It seemed to him and to others that his hand was against everyone — his fellow priests, other prophets, the whole nation, but especially against any who promised peace when he could foresee only "terror on every side."

Jeremiah's own early prophecies were not fulfilled, bringing a crushing disappointment to his young heart and providing reasonable ground for rejection by his contemporaries. For a long while he was silent. He tasted disillusionment at the failure of well-meant efforts at reform, and was repeatedly ridiculed and contradicted by others who claimed to speak for God. He spent a long night in the public stocks, several days in a mud pit, weeks confined to the punishment cells of the city's military guard, and a period in chains. He faced the shattering blows of a good king's sudden death, a bad king's accession and triumph, and the stupid assassination of a promising governor and personal friend. He himself looked death in the face three times, each time being only narrowly rescued.

He spent his later years giving faithful advice to a vacillating king too frightened not to ask for it and too weak to act upon it. And his life ended in humiliation, when he was aged and weak, in enforced exile in the Egypt he had long distrusted, still protesting against the insidious paganism he had fought against all his years. Toward the end he apparently despaired of Judah, feeling that the bond between God and his people had broken at last.

Throughout this prolonged martyrdom, Jeremiah was denied, by God's command, the comfort of wife, family, and home. He was certainly no recluse, for he mentions frequently the "mirth and gladness," the finery and music, of marriage celebrations. The reason for his celibacy recalls that which Saint Paul was to advance later: "I think that in view of the present [gloss reads "impending"] distress it is well for a person to remain as he is" (1 Cor. 7:26); in Jeremiah it would also serve as a living sign to Judah of the sharp distress to come.

Beneath all other sources of pain lay the conviction, almost from the beginning, that his ministry was a lost cause. His message was, "You have no hope but in surrender and exile." "Pray not for this people" was God's verdict more than once; it was too late for repentance. And for Jeremiah himself this conviction was unrelieved by personal hope. He knew of no afterlife that would fulfill and reward the frustrations and disappointments of earthly struggle. He had to endure and obey in the shadowed faith that God would ultimately triumph over his rebellious people in a future in which he himself would never share.

Nor had Jeremiah any inward shield, any psychological shell of defiant pride, aggressive obduracy, or self-righteous indifference to whether people heeded him or not. He was insulated from nothing, vulnerable, mentally and emotionally raw. Among the most moving — and startling — passages in Scripture are Jeremiah's forthright complaints to God, his tender confessions and prayers, mingled with expostulation and challenge, protesting God's having snared him into a prophet's responsibilities, tensions, and anguish.

Yet for over forty years Jeremiah maintained his obedience, reiterated his message, and fulfilled his mission. In the end he sent Judah into exile with no excuses left to hide behind. Such was the measure of his tenacious courage. By so doing, Jeremiah ultimately saved Judah from her worst self, prepared her for a very different future, and proved himself the greatest of the prophets: that is the measure of the man. His greatest achievement was the return of Judah from exile, cleansed from idolatry for all time. His unforgettable legacy was the draft of a new covenant between God and humankind. His priceless memorial is the finest self-disclosure of a saintly soul in the whole Bible.

Tributes

It took time for Jeremiah's full stature to be realized. Almost within his own lifetime, his sayings provided texts for his disciple Ezekiel to echo and elaborate. It is possible to identify some six quotations from the book of Jeremiah in the book of Ezekiel, and perhaps fifteen further "correspondences" in thought. (For examples, cf. Jer. 3:6-18 with Ezek. 23; Jer. 6:27-30 with Ezek. 22:17-22; Jer. 7:16 and 15:1 with Ezek. 14:12-20; Jer. 13:21 with Ezek. 23:22-23; Jer. 18:18 with Ezek. 7:26; Jer. 31:29-30 with Ezek. 18; and the main content of Jer. 31 with Ezek. 36:24-32.) Jeremiah's deep influence upon Ezekiel has a special significance for the date of these particular sayings, and for the way in which Jeremiah's story was preserved by such admirers.

The biblical "Chronicler" blames King Zedekiah for not humbling himself before "Jeremiah the prophet, who spoke from the mouth of the Lord. He also rebelled against King Nebuchad[r]ezzar" (2 Chron. 36:12-13). The latter offense was evidently the less serious! Daniel 9:2 shows the *scriptural* authority ascribed to the book of Jeremiah by the second or third century B.C. About 180 B.C., Ben Sirach noted that the destruction of Jerusalem was in fulfillment of Jeremiah's word, mentioning also the prophet's being persecuted, and quoting the words of Jeremiah's call (Sir. 49:7).

Tributes like these within the Old Testament and the Apocrypha probably explain the rabbinic tradition that places the book of Jeremiah in the Old Testament as the *first* of the prophets, possibly as aptly following the story in 1 and 2 Kings but also implying an authority similar to that of the royal records. Later leaders revered Jeremiah as a mighty intercessor with God. Judas Maccabeus saw in a vision "a man . . . distinguished by his gray hair and dignity, of marvelous majesty and authority . . . a man who loves the brethren, and prays much for the people and the holy city" (2 Macc. 15:13-14).

The long persistence of such disciples and admirers of Jeremiah is of the utmost importance when we come to inquire how the many actions and sayings of the prophet were preserved, and eventually "arranged," in the book we now possess.

"Later generations saw in Jeremiah the supreme prophet,"

says a modern student of the Old Testament, adding, "and rightly." The fine phrase first used of Isaiah has been applied with equal justice to Jeremiah: "His words became history." Says another scholar, "He gave the world more than any other single person in the whole history of Israel." And a third scholar points to the way that Jeremiah saved the central biblical conception of covenanted relationship with God from being submerged in the old Canaanite paganism and the wreck of Israel's national life. He adds, "Humanly speaking, the religious future of the world depended upon this stern and solitary prophet."

So has the reluctant prophet had greatness thrust upon him. He has seriously been reckoned among the authors of the Psalms. And by taking "I appoint you over" (1:10, NIV) as equivalent to "made you overseers" (Acts 20:28, NIV, with the marginal gloss "Traditionally *bishops*"), Jeremiah has been made a church dignitary!

The only fitting appreciation of Jeremiah's person and importance stands upon a far different level. When a later prophet wished to describe the character and fate of the true "servant of the Lord," chosen of God, anointed with his Spirit, it was upon that servant's total rejection, undeserved suffering, and unjust death that he finally dwelt. "Who has believed what we have heard?" Isaiah asks; "And to whom has the arm of the Lord been revealed? . . . He was despised and rejected by men; a man of sorrows, and acquainted with grief. . . . He was bruised for our iniquities; . . . and with his stripes we are healed" (53:1, 3, 5).

So Isaiah sketched his portrait of the coming Servant of the Lord who should save Israel, and in that portrait Jesus himself saw his own lineaments and destiny prefigured. But of whom was Isaiah thinking when he asked his questions? With Jeremiah's story in mind, we may reverently wonder if the words do not describe his experience with astonishing accuracy. And reverent surmise becomes moral certainty when we hear Isaiah at once quote Jeremiah's words about himself: "But I was like a gentle lamb led to the slaughter. I did not know it was against me they devised schemes, saying, . . . 'Let us cut him off from the land of the living'" (Jer. 11:19; cf. Isa. 53:7-8).

And when the coming Servant came, the reluctant prophet received an even greater accolade. Not only did some men say that Jesus *was* Jeremiah (Matt. 16:14), but at the shadowed close of his own ministry it was to the sad, valiant story of Jeremiah's triumphant courage and deathless promise that the thoughts of Jesus turned. In the upper room, on the night on which he was betrayed, Jesus took the Passover cup and gave it to his disciples and quoted Jeremiah: "This cup is *the new covenant* sealed by my blood" (1 Cor. 11:25, NEB, emphasis mine). In that sublime moment all the darkness and rejection, the pain and self-doubt of Jeremiah's life were overlaid with radiance, all his service and suffering hallowed for ever.

A remarkable man indeed!

2

A Wholly Unpropitious Time

If his message is to be relevant, God's spokesman must always
address the situation that confronts him. Besides being well-
informed about peoples and events of his time, Jeremiah was
closely involved with the authorities, personalities, and policies
that controlled the destiny of Judah and shaped the immediate
circumstances, created the prevailing atmosphere, in which he
was called to minister. Yet his thought and his work were
related also to the world and to the future.

Although small in area and remote among her hills, Judah
nevertheless included the city that was to be for centuries the
religious capital of the world, the seedbed of humankind's
loftiest hopes and profoundest beliefs. The little state was part
of the Assyrian province of Syria and Palestine, the cockpit
within which for a thousand years world empires fought for
supremacy. Jeremiah observed and understood what was happening in his world, and became deeply concerned with events
and changes both near and far. Therefore, if we are to understand
his ministry, it is necessary to outline both the wider and the
narrower historical background of his work.

Foreign Affairs

The "cosmic upheaval" into which Jeremiah was born was occasioned by the slow decline, over two centuries, of Assyria, the dominant power of western Asia. From her homeland between the Tigris and the Euphrates (now roughly northern Iraq), Assyria had held sway from the Persian Gulf to the Aegean Sea and south to the borders of Egypt, holding her many provinces either under direct rule and occupation, or (like Judah) as obedient, tribute-paying neighbors.

But by Jeremiah's time, Assyria's power was waning, undermined by internal dissension, intrigue, resentment against tyranny, and moral exhaustion. Seizing their opportunity, savage hordes of Scythian marauders from the Black Sea area had, for some thirty years, flooded into Asia Minor and Syria, compelling Assyria to disperse her defensive forces. The Greek historian Herodotus says the Scythians drove as far south as Egypt. As occasion offered, Egypt too, always ready to assert a right to Palestine, threatened Assyria's borders from the south.

About the time of Jeremiah's call, more Scythians were on the move from the west, while the eastern province of Chaldea was stirring with ambition. Assyria's capital city, massive Nineveh (a hundred miles north of modern Baghdad), was captured by the Chaldean insurgents in 612 B.C., and the city of Babylon, nearer to the Persian Gulf, became the new focus of world empire.

Fearing that Assyria's conquerors might prove a still more powerful foe, Egypt moved northward, as though to support Assyria, reaching Megiddo, near Carmel, in 609 B.C. There Josiah, king of Judah, met Egypt's Pharaoh Neco, apparently seeking to reassert his own claim to northern Israel. But he was killed, though whether he died in battle or was assassinated is not clear (2 Kings 23:29-30; 2 Chron. 35:20-27). Egypt pressed northward to Carchemish (near the northeastern corner of the Mediterranean), where in 605 B.C. all her hope of ruling Palestine was crushed by the Chaldeans under Nebuchadrezzar (604-561 B.C.). For the rest of Jeremiah's life the Chaldeans ruled the Near East from ancient and beautiful Babylon. It is customary, and simpler, to call them "the Babylonians" henceforth.

The ministry of Jeremiah in Judah was inevitably interwoven with these distant events. The Scythian threat most probably evoked his earliest preaching. At Josiah's death, Egypt appointed Judah's next king, Jehoiakim, who eventually died while attempting to withstand a Babylonian siege. Dual pressures naturally created in Jerusalem a pro-Babylon party and a pro-Egypt party, each seeking by foreign support to retain a minimum of independence. Jeremiah did not believe that either policy offered any real hope for faithless Judah.

Babylon took into exile Judah's next king, Jehoiachin, along with a number of leading Jews, leaving Zedekiah on the throne. When he too proved unreliable, Babylon lost patience, destroyed Jerusalem, carried king, nobles, and people into exile, and left the almost empty countryside to a few impoverished peasants. Jeremiah was left in the charge of a provincial governor, and when he was assassinated, the remaining Jews carried Jeremiah against his will to Egypt. There he died, at the close of a period so disturbed and confused that no man of sensitive spirit could ever wish to be a prophet in such a time.

Jeremiah was aware that God's hand was behind the rise and fall of empires, the actions of Egypt, Syria, and Philistia, the destiny of Moab, Edom, and Ammon, and was shaping the developing history of Judah, Assyria, and Babylon. He could say to an "official" prophet, Hananiah, "The prophets who preceded you and me from ancient times prophesied war, famine, and pestilence against many countries and great kingdoms" (28:8). In his interpretation of world events and their consequences, Jeremiah revealed clearer vision and deeper insight than all his predecessors.

He well understood that for Judah the whole aspect of the world had changed. But to his mind the earth was the Lord's, the world and all who dwell therein. He faithfully represents the far-reaching message of the whole prophetic movement in Israel: that the God of Abraham, Isaac, and Jacob is not merely the God of Israel but the Lord of history and of the whole earth.

Home Affairs

Inevitably, Jeremiah was much more deeply and personally concerned with the life, politics, sins, and tragedy of his own people. He was "concerned" rather than "involved," since his counsel, influence, and warnings were constantly rejected, and he was forced to remain a frustrated spectator of approaching catastrophe. The disappearance of northern Israel presented to Judah a stark example of what could happen to a "chosen" people who forfeited God's favor. Such warning was needed, for Judah had just emerged from the long, evil reign of Manasseh (approximately 696-641 B.C.), prolonged but not mitigated by the two-year rule of his son, Amon.

Manasseh had reacted violently against the religious reforms introduced by his father, Hezekiah. He encouraged again, alongside acknowledgment of the God of the patriarchs, the worship of fertility spirits ("Baals") — sacramental prostitution (male and female) to promote fecundity of soil, flocks, and families, and ritual drunkenness to honor the Baals of the vineyards. Infant sacrifice also was resumed, presumably in times of stress (cf. 2 Kings 16:2-3). Manasseh even burned his own son "as an offering" (2 Kings 21:6).

The full list of Manasseh's "abominable practices" given in 2 Kings 21 includes most of the practices of the ancient Canaanite cults — wizardry and witchcraft, necromancy, soothsaying, augury, the worship of Asherah. "Asherah" was probably

originally a wooden pole symbolizing deity, and later a stone
pillar graven to represent the Canaanite goddess Ishtar, or
Astarte. Such had been erected in Israel by King Ahab under
Phoenician influence, and were now restored. Ishtar, the mother
goddess or "queen of heaven," was worshipped all over the Middle
East, from Babylon to Egypt, under various names, besides
"Anath" and "Anath-yahu" (cf. 44:19).

As vassal to Assyria, Manasseh was obliged to acknowledge also the sun-god Shamash, with his symbolic chariots and
the "host of heaven," the moon and stars. Meanwhile, the
Jerusalem temple was sorely neglected, as the extensive repair
required in Josiah's time plainly reveals. Any resistance to
Manasseh's revival of paganism, offered by disciples of the earlier prophets, was punished by death (2 Kings 21:16). A tradition preserved in the apocryphal "Ascension of Isaiah" and
referred to in Hebrews 11:37 says that Isaiah of Jerusalem was
at this time "sawn asunder" (KJV).

This account of Manasseh's wickedness is confirmed by
Zephaniah (a prophet contemporary with Jeremiah; see Zeph.
1:4-6, 8), by reiterated condemnation (Jer. 15:4; 2 Kings 21:9, 16,
17, 20; 23:12, 26; 24:3), and by the king's later reputation as
having presided over the worst period in the religious life of Judah.
The sole contrary record is at 2 Chronicles 33:10-20. This tells of
the punishment of Manasseh at Babylon (his "visit" to Babylon
has some support in extra-biblical records), and of his subsequent
conversion and reparations at Jerusalem. The only explanation of
this single contrary judgment so far offered (and an unwelcome
one) is that the Chronicler desired to find edifying lessons in the
awful history of that reign, if only to account for what certain
scholars have called "the longest reign of the worst of kings."

Thus, religiously as well as politically, it was the worst of
times in which to become a prophet. Yet the spiritual darkness
was not entirely unrelieved. Before Jeremiah began to prophesy,
the young Josiah, only eight years of age, followed Manasseh

and Amon on the throne, and in the new king the reforming zeal of his great-grandfather Hezekiah soon showed itself. He began to seek the God of David when he was only sixteen, and at twenty he set about purging his kingdom (2 Chron. 34:1-7).

Josiah's Reform

2 Kings 23 tells how, when Jeremiah had been prophesying for about five years, Josiah turned his attention to the repair of the neglected temple, and was informed of the discovery there of a book of the divine law. This contained regulations plainly new to that generation and added warnings of punishment that deeply disturbed the king and his supporters. They consulted not Jeremiah but a prophetess named Huldah. Jeremiah was, after all, only about the king's own age, and little known; besides, he belonged to that priestly circle which fostered the hill shrines condemned by this book. Huldah advised immediate obedience to the regulations.

Penetrating self-examination, widespread correction of abuses, and several liturgical innovations followed speedily. Negatively, the "high places" and fertility cults, the shrines dedicated to the host of heaven, the roof altars to the sun, the shrine of Molech associated with infant sacrifice — all were proscribed or destroyed. Compromising priests, cult prostitutes, wizards, and necromancers were removed, even assassinated. The reforming crusade was thorough and prolonged.

Positively, king and people returned to the roots of national religious life in an elaborate and formal act of reconsecration, reading in public the new "Book of the Covenant" and vowing to fulfill its statutes. Thus Josiah sought to reestablish the ancient covenant relationship of God and Israel, the people freely pledging their obedience to the terms upon which God offered security, prosperity, and blessing.

Henceforward all sacrificial worship was to be centralized at the temple in Jerusalem, under direct "official" control. The hill shrines were to be abandoned. A national Passover festival was instituted, celebrated in the temple and not in the homes of the people as hitherto. (2 Kings 23:22 emphasizes this innovation; provision was made for the maintenance of unemployed country priests and for the meat of animals not slaughtered at the local altars to be available in the villages; see 2 Kings 23; 2 Chron. 34 and 35.)

Almost every feature of Josiah's reform corresponds with commands and warnings familiar to us in the book of Deuteronomy, or "second law," especially the centralization of worship and the emphasis upon covenant relationship with God. This suggests that the book found in the temple was a version, summary, or reissue of our book of Deuteronomy. But its values, themes, language, and style are characteristic of the prophetic "movement" known to us in Amos, Micah, Hosea, Isaiah of Jerusalem, and Jeremiah, with their demand for pure religion, individual righteousness, social justice, abandonment of idolatry, and wide and sensitive humanitarianism.

Josiah's reform evidently represents a temporary supremacy of the outlook of the greater prophets. Although not explicitly mentioned by Jeremiah, it was undoubtedly the most promising event in his lifetime — and perhaps the most disappointing. For his own attitude to it is the subject of thorough and persistent questioning.

Jeremiah's concern over Judah's internal politics increased as the situation she faced grew more desperate. The sudden death of Josiah changed everything. Jeremiah continued to proclaim the divine will on all matters affecting Judah's welfare, counseled her rulers, and commented publicly on actions taken and the dangers that threatened, though he was rarely heard with patience. During the reign of Judah's last king he became the secret counselor of the throne, advising surrender to Babylon while reasonable terms could still be negotiated. Inevitably he became the target of the "false prophets" and the pro-Egypt party, and was suspected by many of treacherous support of the state's enemies.

Jeremiah's Aim

Yet in all this public and "political" ministry Jeremiah was no social activist or power-seeking politician. It was his destiny to prophesy under five very different kings and to watch his beloved people's steady drift to disaster. *Josiah* was pious, well-intentioned but not over-wise, and came to the throne — and to his death — too soon. *Jehoahaz* lasted only three months, though evil possibilities were already recognized in him in that short span. *Jehoiakim* was deliberately wicked, extravagant, and malicious. Like Jehoahaz, *Jehoiachin* was king for only three months, and might have developed either well or ill. *Zedekiah* balanced weakness and folly in equal proportions.

For Josiah, Jeremiah had respect; for Jehoahaz, regret. Toward Jehoiakim he showed outright opposition, and for Jehoiachin, sympathy. To Zedekiah, Jeremiah showed considerable understanding mingled with firmness. Among them all, Jeremiah alone preserved a consistent policy, a steadfast character, a clear-eyed realism, and a persistent struggle to maintain faith and loyalty toward God.

In the end he shared fully the bitterness of a long siege and total defeat. Twice he witnessed the heartbreaking removal of Judah's leading people, including his own friends. He suffered the severe disappointment of the senseless murder of the one man who could have made life tolerable in the ruined land. Faced with the renewed idolatries of the remnant of the Jews in Egypt, he suffered the final rejection of his ministry and surrendered his faith in Judah — but not his faith in God, and so not his faith in the future.

However, to imagine that Jeremiah's personal disappointments and frustrations add up to the failure of his mission is to miss altogether the main purpose of his life and ministry. As has been hinted at already, the meaning of Jeremiah's work must be read in the light of the long years that followed. The changes in the disposition of world power meant that Judah — weakened by dissension, meddling in events beyond her control, and faithless to her God — could not escape defeat. Since it was Babylon's policy to remove troublesome people from their homelands, defeat meant exile. Jeremiah knew that doom was sealed.

In consequence, a most painful mission of preparation was essential, and someone had to fulfill it. Resistance to Babylon would be hopeless; surrender alone could limit the bloodshed and ruin. But to counsel surrender was held to be treason — and against God's people, blasphemy.

Yet if Judah went into exile blaming the past, or the fathers, or fate, or foreigners, or God, then the experience would teach her nothing and would only breed bitterness and further rebelliousness. But if she went forth in true sorrow, feeling her guilt before God, and in her suffering found the way to penitence, then the outcome could yet be healing, cleansing, and the renewal of her covenant with God. A generation or two immersed in the heathenism she had so long lusted after might well cure her of it forever. If her humiliation was rightly interpreted as God's cleansing judgment, Judah might yet return with God's law written upon her heart.

Jeremiah believed that possible. To prepare for it was his task.

The Exile largely achieved this purpose. Judah was never again seriously tempted to emulate pagan ways. Instead, in the Maccabean age she resisted heroically all attempts of foreign conquerors to impose alien customs upon her, and she has done so ever since. That outstanding trait in the Jewish character is traceable, historically, to Jeremiah's indomitable faithfulness in laying the true causes of Judah's disaster squarely upon Judah's conscience.

It was a thankless task in a wholly unpropitious age, especially for one so lonely, so sensitive, so vulnerable — and so reluctant. Yet beyond question he was God's chosen man for that daunting, tumultuous time.

3

An Oddly Confusing Book

To be strictly accurate, the book of Jeremiah is "oddly confusing" only to those who persist in reading it as it was never meant to be read — that is, those who read it straight through as an orderly, coherent story of Jeremiah's life and preaching. It is not that kind of book.

The book of Jeremiah is richly rewarding to dip into. It is full of stimulating insights: "They have healed the wound of my people lightly, saying, 'Peace, peace,' when there is no peace" (6:14); "Their idols are like scarecrows in a cucumber field, and they cannot speak; they have to be carried, for they cannot walk. Be not afraid of them, for they cannot do evil; neither is it in them to do good" (10:5); "He judged the cause of the poor and needy. . . . Is not this to know me? says the Lord" (22:16); "Let the prophet who has a dream tell the dream, but let him who has my word speak my word faithfully. What has straw in common with wheat? . . . Is not my word like fire . . . and like a hammer which breaks the rock in pieces?" (23:28-29). And there is much more of this kind.

The book contains many arresting phrases and images.

"Can a maiden forget her ornaments, or a bride her attire? Yet my people have forgotten me days without number" (2:32); "Even the stork . . . knows her times; and the turtledove, swallow, and crane keep the time of their coming; but my people know not the ordinance of the Lord" (8:7); "If you have raced with men on foot, and they have wearied you, how will you compete with horses? And if in a safe land you fall down, how will you do in the jungle of the Jordan?" (12:5); "The Lord said to me: 'Do not pray for the welfare of this people'" (14:11); "Then I said, 'Ah, Lord God, surely thou hast utterly deceived this people and Jerusalem, saying, "It shall be well with you"; whereas the sword has reached their very life'" (4:10); "Babylon was a golden cup in the Lord's hand, making all the earth drunken" (51:7); "Moab has been at ease from his youth and has settled on his lees; . . . Therefore, behold, the days are coming, says the Lord, when I shall send to him tilters who will tilt him" (48:11-12); "Am I a God at hand, says the Lord, and not a God afar off?" (23:23). — And many more.

The book of Jeremiah contains — besides its splendid poetry, dramatic events, and exciting stories kindling the imagination — a host of fine texts for useful preaching: 5:1; 29:11; 10:23; chapters 13 and 31 — the list could be endless. Altogether, it is an excellent book for browsing, a rewarding book to study. But . . .

Surveying the Book

The alert reader finds his interest constantly rekindled and his heart moved, but when he attempts to read the book through, other impressions obtrude. The first, in all probability, will be that the book is very disjointed. Innumerable rapid, unexplained changes of subject often make the connection between verses obscure. Hardly a chapter does not bewilder us at some

point, leaving us striving to see, or to invent, a coherence that
is not there. Modern translations often warn us of such discon-
tinuity, but not frequently enough.

The second impression will probably be of disorder.
Noting just eight chapters in their printed order — 21, 24, 25,
26, 27, 29, 32, and 35 — confirms this impression: their opening words flit from the time of Zedekiah to the beginning of
the first exile, back to the reign of Jehoiakim, then to a period
earlier in his reign, then again to Zedekiah, then to the time
after the first exiles reached Babylon, then to the tenth year of
Zedekiah, and again back to Jehoiakim. There are many more
instances of this seemingly haphazard arrangement. For one
more example: at chapters 46-51 we might suppose that
Jeremiah has, at the end, abandoned Judah's problems to concentrate on those of her neighbors. But careful analysis shows
that a great deal in these chapters belongs not to the end but
to the days of Jehoiakim, when Jeremiah had much more still
to say to Judah.

If the reader is not only alert but retentive, he or she will
soon discover, and be teased by, numerous repetitions. Among
them are the following: 6:22-24 (addressed to Zion) is repeated
at 50:41-43 (addressed to Babylon); 49:18-21 (against Edom)
is echoed at 50:40, 44-46 (adapted for Babylon); 22:11-12
repeats in prose the substance of the poem at 22:10; chapter
26 tells from another viewpoint the story already told in 7:1-15;
the substance of 31:35-37 (poetry) recurs at 33:19-22 (prose).

There are a host of other repetitions: 6:12-15 = 8:10-12;
7:31-33 = 19:5-7 (adapted); 8:15 = 14:19; 10:12-16 = 51:15-
19; 11:20 = 20:12; 15:13-14 = 17:3-4; 16:14-15 = 23:7-8;
23:19-20 = 30:23-24; 30:10-11 = 46:27-28 (adapted); 39:1-2
condenses 52:4-7; 49:26 = 50:30; compare also 2:28 with
11:13. Surely Jeremiah could not have been so forgetful of what
he himself had already written. Nor does such internal repetition exhaust the puzzles. For 52:1-27, 31-34 repeats 2 Kings

24:18–25:21, 27-30; and 49:14-16, 9 combines two "oracles" also attributed to Obadiah (Obad. 1-5), the words being treasured when (apparently) the original authorship had become uncertain. All this curious repetition must be borne in mind when we ask how the book of Jeremiah came to be put together.

Reading observantly, one also becomes aware of a striking variety of material in the book, in addition to the mixture of prose and poetry. Nearly a third of the book (420 verses out of 1,379) is not by Jeremiah but about him. These passages report what he said, thought, or did, as observed by an onlooker or learned later by a disciple. And chapter 52 does not even mention Jeremiah — chapter 51 ends, explicitly, with "Thus far are the words of Jeremiah." Chapter 52 has thus the nature of an appendix, completing the story. The final paragraph of the book recounts events that Jeremiah did not live to see.

Many other passages are uttered by Jeremiah of himself (for examples, contrast 14:11, 15:1, and 16:1 with 14:1, 18:1, and 21:1). Most of these are "prophetic utterances," frequently with the interjection "Thus saith the Lord" or "The word [literally 'oracle'] of the Lord." These oracles are often in poetic form, though some twenty-nine now have prose "headings" and dates attached. These introductions are by someone reporting: for example, 14:1 begins with "The word of the Lord which came *to Jeremiah,*" not *"to me."* Still other passages are dictated by Jeremiah, as were those to Baruch the scribe, recalling what he had said at an earlier time. Yet other passages pursue thoughts, offer prayers, or record "conversations" with God that only Jeremiah could have revealed.

From even this cursory survey of the book's contents — memoirs, divine oracles, soliloquies and prayers, a historical appendix, matter dictated by the prophet, reminiscences treasured by others, all assembled with little chronological or logical order, and with considerable repetition — it becomes clear that *the book is confusing to read straight through simply because it was not written consecutively.* The book itself has had a history, a process of production.

The book of Jeremiah is in fact a collection, an anthology, of memories, utterances, and events, gathered in stages from different periods in Jeremiah's long ministry and afterward, and arranged, so far as it is arranged at all, with more regard to themes and literary connections than to historical order. That simple insight into how the book came into being yields surprising help toward understanding it.

The Preservation of Prophecy

It is well to recall that earlier prophets like Samuel, Nathan, Elijah, Elisha, and Micaiah did not (so far as we know) leave written records of their ministries. Occasional commands to write (Isa. 8:1, 16; 30:8) imply that writing was not usual. In a largely illiterate society, family and tribal records were kept, with astonishing accuracy, in the prodigious memories of successive generations, helped sometimes by poetic form and by vivid visual imagery. Compare the persistence of folk tales, folk music, nursery rhymes, Homer's poems, and the histories of Herodotus.

In religious circles, communities or "schools" of disciples or devotees treasured the stories and sayings of their heroes, usually by oral repetition. We hear of "the sons of the prophets" (2 Kings 2:3, 5, etc.), the "disciples" of Isaiah (Isa. 8:16). With the passing of generations, the rivalries of schools, persecution, and alien pressures, it became advisable to record what otherwise might be lost. The "collection" and recording of memoirs and oracles attributable to revered teachers became the task of their disciples, and continued as long as new material could be found. The books of Isaiah, Zechariah, and especially Jeremiah bear clear marks of this process.

In the case of the book of Jeremiah, however, we have it on the prophet's own authority that his earlier prophecies, uttered over more than twenty years, were written down during his lifetime, long after they were delivered. Chapter 36 tells us that Baruch the scribe was commissioned for this task in order *to communicate* Jeremiah's message to the leaders of the people when Jeremiah himself was barred from the temple. After Jehoiakim burned the first copy, Baruch wrote the whole again, and "many similar words were added" (36:32). This second copy appears to have been for purposes of *record*.

There is little doubt that Baruch's record is, for the years it covered, one of the principal sources of the present "Jeremiah collection." But we must allow for some additions — the "similar words added" — and for some revision due to later reflection or to later knowledge of events. In a few places, we can almost hear Baruch reporting and can discern the modifications due to hindsight. Baruch continued with Jeremiah to the end in Egypt (43:6-7), doubtless still adding to his scroll.

And the growth of the Jeremiah memoirs continued for a long time. When, about 250 B.C., the Greek version of the Old Testament was produced in Alexandria, its text of Jeremiah (and the Hebrew text on which it was based?) was 2,700 words shorter than our Hebrew copies. In addition, "our" chapters 46-51 are in a different order; and, strangest of all, they replace 25:14, following the words "Jeremiah prophesied against all the nations." Evidently these "oracles against foreign nations" once existed as a separate collection, which the Hebrew scribes, and later the Greek, inserted in places they considered appropriate. We shall see reason for thinking that someone similarly formed an anthology of Jeremiah's prophecies concerning the distant future. It seems clear that even so late, neither the text nor the arrangement of the Jeremiah collection was yet unalterably settled.

What seems certain, amid much "probability," is that

various disciples or groups continued to treasure and collect memoirs and utterances of their beloved prophet long after his death. The New English Bible boldly incorporates this opinion within the text, by paraphrasing 51:64 as "Thus far are the *collected* sayings of Jeremiah" (italics mine).

So prolonged a process of compilation explains readily the book's curious features, like the variety of materials used. We do not expect an anthology of isolated memories to read smoothly like a continuous story, or to observe strict historical sequence. Repetitions naturally occur, as different collectors preserve varying versions of the same event or saying. Famous words spoken about Edom easily come to be attributed to either Jeremiah or Obadiah with the passage of time, and the same lapse of time explains why 33:14-16 so closely resembles the post-exilic passages in Zechariah 3:8 and 6:12, and why 10:1-16 reflects the experience of Judah in Babylon, which Jeremiah did not share. The enthusiasm of collectors of prized hero-memories sometimes outruns their vigilance.

Studying the Result

It is tempting to liken the book of Jeremiah to a box of jigsaw pieces that need to be re-assembled in proper order, by hints of shape, color, and emerging pattern, before the portrait of a very great man slowly becomes clear. More appropriately, perhaps, the book of Jeremiah resembles a scrapbook of undated memories and snapshots recalling great moments in a splendid life, over which we pore one by one, with reverence, saying, "Ah, that must have been when . . ."

The simple truth is that the book of Jeremiah confronts the earnest reader with a choice: either to read through the book as it is, with all its repetitions and sudden changes, trying to keep the story straight in his mind; or to put the story of Jeremiah into its correct order (so far as possible) and to fit the collected reminiscences of his sayings and deeds into that chronological outline. The present study attempts — though with varying degrees of confidence — the second process, fitting the pieces of the jigsaw into the coherent pattern that they seem to imply.

Such a method of Bible study demands a little explanation:

(i)   We first note carefully where a passage is not connected with its present context, especially when what goes before and what comes after is clearer without it.

(ii)   Within such an "island" passage we seek clues to where it may belong in the whole story by the names, places, or events alluded to, or by the thoughts, words, and phrases that closely resemble those of other passages of which we already know the date.

(iii)   In piecing together Jeremiah's story, we seek help from other scriptures — 2 Kings, 2 Chronicles, and elsewhere.

(iv)   Hesitantly, we assume that the defeat and destruction of Jerusalem and the consequent exile became *more* rather than less clear to Jeremiah as the events drew nearer — affording another possible clue to the date of some sayings.

(v)   We conclude that verses which now occur together do not necessarily belong together, and that passages which are separated may belong together. The compilers put alongside Jeremiah's breaking of an earthen jar the story of his visit to the potter, though there is no inner connection of meaning or date; the separation of two accounts of the same event (chapters 7 and 26) and of chapter 45 from chapter 36 means nothing more than that that is how the material came into the collectors' hands.

Despite the greatest diligence, some passages remain undatable. The final test of all suggestions and theories is the light thrown upon the text, liberating its meaning. The reader should try to accept what rings true, to *weigh the reasons* offered for any suggestion, to suspend judgment where unconvinced, and to ignore anything that merely bewilders.

Two other "problems" should be recognized. First, the meaning of some Hebrew words is unknown; other ancient versions (Syriac, Greek, the Latin Vulgate, the Hebrew paraphrases in common speech — the Targums) sometimes differ from the Hebrew manuscripts; and sometimes the Hebrew manuscripts differ among themselves where copyists appear to have blundered. In modern translations, footnotes usually warn of any important variations. Thousands of informed judgments lie behind every new translation, but translation is an art, not a science, and all dogmatism is excluded. Care, integrity, a sincere desire always to understand (and never to distort) God's Word must be assumed. But unwelcome facts and awkward literary or historical judgments have to be faced with honesty.

Second, Jeremiah seems often to add brief "closing" words of hope and comfort that unexpectedly weaken a clear prophecy of punishment and doom (46:27-28; 48:47; 49:6, 39 are but a few examples). Would Jeremiah so "take back" the stern words he had just uttered? And if he did, need he have been persecuted? Are these "hopeful closures" the product of hindsight — the compilers knowing that the dreadful things foretold did not happen quite that way? Or a pastoral encouragement meant to preserve faith in dark days? Or examples of Jeremiah's faith breaking through clouded skies? Or examples of a rabbinic habit to close public reading of harsh passages with a cheering, hopeful verse from the Psalms (such hopeful remarks later becoming attached to Jeremiah's messages)? Each example must be considered in the light of all possibilities.

Those who find such questions and such disciplines of study unwelcome might ponder that deepest of all Christian principles — truth through *incarnation*. The book of Jeremiah was not penned by angels, did not fall ready-written in all languages from the skies. It was given to the world, as all God's gifts are given, in and through the normal processes of life — in this instance, through the ordinary processes of communication, speech, memory, penmanship, collecting, copying, translating, and printing.

A spiritual genius, a moral giant, a man of God who was also a vulnerable soul of intense integrity wrestled with God in a disastrous age and spoke God's truth about it. Devoted followers preserved and assembled his memoirs as best they could. So God revealed his mind in that time for all time and for all similar situations. And the process by which the revelation came is part of the truth itself, the manifestation of what is divine and eternal through what is human and temporary: *for only so can we grasp it.*

4

A Very Full Cast

Forty years on the public stage is a long career and must involve a large company of fellow players. The book of Jeremiah is so crowded with varied people that some sorting out is necessary and proves informative. The similarity of names can be confusing; there are twenty in the book that end in the short name for God, "iah" — among them are Jeremiah ("God-founded"), Josiah ("God heals"), Zedekiah ("rightness of God"), Hananiah ("God is gracious"), and Zephaniah ("God protects").

Equally confusing is the custom of repeating a family name through several generations for grandfathers, fathers, sons, and cousins and their sons. Epithets might distinguish individual members ("Uriah of Kiriath-jearim," "Hananiah the prophet"), but more frequent is the tedious recital of a man's genealogy through three or four generations (e.g., "Ishmael the son of Nethaniah, son of Elishama, of the royal family").

To miss such details leads to muddle. Seraiah son of Azriel was not Seraiah son of Neriah, Seraiah son of Azariah, or Seraiah son of Tanhumeth, all of whom are mentioned in the book of Jeremiah. Gemariah son of Shaphan was not Gemariah son of

Hilkiah, nor (almost certainly) was that Gemariah a brother to Jeremiah, though both were sons of a "Hilkiah." That was a common priestly name. Jeremiah the prophet was not the grandfather of Zedekiah the king (52:1), nor a founder of the house of Rechab (35:3); there are nine "Jeremiahs" in the Old Testament. One more example: Zephaniah the prophet (son of Cushi) was Jeremiah's contemporary, but not identical with Zephaniah the priest (son of Ma-aseiah), who had a brother called Zedekiah who *was* a prophet and not the prince Zedekiah (son of Hananiah) or the king Zedekiah (son of Josiah)!

These few examples show the need for caution and for attempting to put some flesh on the chief members of this cast with outlandish names.

Jeremiah's Kings

For the present, enough has been said about Manasseh and Amon, and about Josiah, Jehoiakim, and Zedekiah, who come on stage at once (1:1-3) and occupy its center in turn. Jehoahaz (whom Jeremiah for some reason calls "Shallum") and Jehoia-chin (whom Jeremiah three times calls "Coniah," and four times "Jeconiah") merely cross the footlights. To make things doubly bewildering, it must be added that Jehoiakim began life as Eliakim, and Zedekiah began as Mattaniah. When foreign over-lords appointed puppet kings, they changed the kings' names to emphasize their vassal status. These particular complications are best ignored.

Of foreign rulers who enter Judah's drama, mention must be made of Pharaoh Neco of Egypt (610-595 B.C.), who saw Josiah killed at Megiddo and was himself soundly defeated by the "Babylonians" at Carchemish. And of Pharaoh Hophra (589-570 B.C.), grandson of Neco, who by assisting Zedekiah to attempt revolt against Babylon (Ezek. 17:11-18) occasioned the final destruction of Jerusalem. He apparently sent relief to Jerusalem during the siege (37:5), and received the remnant of fugitives from Jerusalem into Egypt (44:28-30).

However, the most powerful of foreign rulers to affect Judah was Nebuchadrezzar (sometimes miscalled "Nebuchadnezzar"), described in the book of Jeremiah twenty-seven times as "king of Babylon," and once — surprisingly — as God's "servant" (43:10). Nebuchadrezzar consolidated the rule of the province of Babylon over the whole former empire of Assyria, beginning at Carchemish (in 605 B.C.). In 561 B.C. he passed the throne to his son Evil Merodach. ("Evil" is a forename, not an adjective!) From his own annals it appears that Nebuchadrezzar was prouder of his buildings and fortifications than of his victories, but "he certainly was the greatest king of Babylon since Hammurabi" (of about 1800 B.C.).

The officer commanding Nebuchadrezzar's campaign against Jerusalem was Nebuzaradan, captain of the bodyguards. He delivered the leading captives to Nebuchadrezzar at Riblah in northern Syria, superintended the evacuation of the exiles to Babylon, allotted land to the poorest people remaining, and appointed a Jewish nobleman, Gedaliah, to be governor of Judea. Nebuzaradan also, on the king's orders, made arrangements for the care and relative freedom of aged Jeremiah, and of the Jewish king's young daughters. He was an efficient soldier, and a wise and kindly official.

Jeremiah's Friends

This Gedaliah (contrast 38:1) must certainly be reckoned among Jeremiah's most loyal friends. He represents the third generation of a family of "princes" who supported Jeremiah against popular hostility. Shaphan, a state secretary under Josiah and an active supporter of Josiah's reform, had three sons:

Ahikam helped in the reform, and later intervened courageously to save Jeremiah from Jehoiakim and the fickle crowd (26:24); Elasah carried a dangerous letter for Jeremiah to exiles already in Babylon (29:3); and Gemariah lent his office in the temple for the first reading of Baruch's scroll, heard the second reading, and pleaded with the king not to burn the document. It was one of Gemariah's sons, Micaiah, who first warned that Baruch's scroll was politically dangerous (36:10-13, 25). Another of Gemariah's sons was Gedaliah.

It was doubtless this valiant and loyal family's support of Jeremiah's "surrender and be saved" policy that led to Gedaliah's appointment as provincial governor when Jerusalem fell. Certain other princes followed the lead of this family of Shaphan against the persecuting prophets and priests, and later gathered around Gedaliah. He was soon murdered by a jealous rival, but the high honor in which he and his family came to be held was expressed in solemn remembrance of his death in one of the four main fasts of the Jewish year.

38:6-13; 39:15-18   In one of the shining cameos of the Old Testament is enshrined the striking portrait of a most unexpected friend of Jeremiah, as courageous as Shaphan's princely sons and as important in saving Jeremiah's life, but a very different individual, a black slave. Enraged at the "seditious" counsel of Jeremiah, four nobles demanded his death. Weak Zedekiah gave abject acquiescence. So Jeremiah was let down into an "empty" cistern — empty, that is, except for mud, which (it is said) would not deserve mention in the ancient east unless it were waist-deep.

Such treatment spelled certain death from exposure and starvation (38:9), without actual violence or indictable murder (cf. Gen. 37:20-24). Probably no individual was brave enough to strike a physical blow against a prophet, or to risk his own life by defending him. The foreign slave, Ebed-melech, with immense courage, reported Jeremiah's situation directly to the king, thus involving the throne in responsibility if Jeremiah died. Receiving the king's permission and the help of three men (so the RSV says; the NIV says "thirty," surely a crowd for a secret operation), Ebed-melech hauled the old prophet out of the pit and into the safety of the palace's former guardroom.

One exquisite detail in this simple story is Ebed-melech's gentleness: he provided "old rags and worn-out clothes" to protect Jeremiah's arms as he was raised. Another is that Ebed-melech was, in contrast with the nobles, essentially a "nobody," a Cushite alien (Nubian? Ethiopian?), a captured, kidnapped, or purchased slave, emasculated for the purposes of guarding the king's harem (or for military duties, possibly in honor of a god) — on all counts socially unacceptable, unable to join Judah, banned from the temple, yet truly heroic in loyalty, courage, and compassion. He may even be anonymous, if "Ebed-melech" means only "one of the servants of the king" (as it might), possibly a designation used to help ensure his own safety afterward.

Jeremiah understood and appreciated fully what the man had done, his fears and his fine qualities. For he sent Ebed-melech a word from God assuring him that though he would see the destruction of Jerusalem, his life would be spared, both from the nobles' revenge and in the final battle. (The RSV's "you shall have your life as a prize of war" probably means "as the spoil by which you will be rewarded"; the NEB finds in the words a promise that Ebed-melech will return home.) Even more precious to the alien slave would be the recognition and acceptance implied in Jeremiah's words, "because you have put your trust in me, says the Lord."

> *Reflection:* Zedekiah, a king, is "a perfect monument of the miseries that wait upon weakness," and a slave in spirit; Ebed-melech — alien, exile, and slave — is a splendid example of the courage born of faith, and a prince in spirit.

Among Jeremiah's younger admirers was Ezekiel, perhaps thirty years his junior. Since Jeremiah does not mention him, "friend" seems too strong a description, but Ezekiel later became an ardent disciple, preserving many reminiscences of Jeremiah's teaching. Both a priest and a prophet like Jeremiah, Ezekiel ministered in Jerusalem for a few years before its fall, and later in Babylon.

36:4-19, 26, 32; 45 Closest of all to Jeremiah through some twenty years was Baruch, the scribe or secretary. Himself one of the nobles of Judah, he had their attention when he read the scroll of Jeremiah's prophecies in the temple, and he obeyed their counsel to take Jeremiah into hiding while they approached King Jehoiakim with the prophet's message. Baruch and Jeremiah were so closely associated in the public mind as to justify the description "Baruch the secretary and Jeremiah the prophet" (36:26).

During the prophet's later persecution, Baruch's social position evidently protected him, but Baruch remained loyal, publicly witnessing a deed of purchase when Jeremiah bought a field (32:12-16) and remaining with Jeremiah alongside Gedaliah when the city fell. That he was blamed for exercising too great an influence on the aging prophet is a significant tribute to the value Jeremiah placed upon him. Baruch was still with Jeremiah upon their enforced arrival in Egypt.

Such loyalty at such a time was costly. In the whole Old Testament there is no personal note quite like that which, during that dangerous confrontation with angry Jehoiakim, Jeremiah dictated to Baruch (chap. 45). Baruch had evidently been expressing his grief and anxiety for them both, and for the future of Judah, confessing some weariness of spirit. After all, as a prince in Israel, Baruch had some right to expect a prosperous, easy, influential life, but instead he found himself sharing Jeremiah's rejection.

Jeremiah replied that the breaking down and uprooting

of Judah was neither merely an accident nor the triumph of
human wickedness but the Lord's doing. The Lord who first
built and planted the nation was still "watching over his word
to perform it" (cf. 1:12). But amid God's judgments in evil
days, individuals may have to pay dearly for loyalty to God. It
was no time for Baruch to seek great things for himself. But
Jeremiah promised that Baruch would be spared to live on when
present storms were past — his life, like spoils in battle, would
be given him as a reward for valor. Baruch evidently treasured
that note of gracious reassurance, since he added it long afterward to his collection of his hero's sayings.

> *Reflection:* Prosperity, security, and peace are legitimate
> ambitions even for people of God, but they are not
> "rights," and they may have to be surrendered when
> God or conscience so require.

26:20-23   We could wish to know more of one who shared
Jeremiah's views and policy and died for that in complete obscurity. All that is known of Uriah of Kiriath-jearim is recorded in
this curious footnote to history. A prophet, he denounced Judah's
ways, incurred Jehoiakim's anger, fled to Egypt, was hounded,
and was brought back and executed. Even that brief reference is
recalled only to point to how this episode contrasts with the way
King Hezekiah had treated Micah, in similar circumstances, and
so to illustrate the danger in which Jeremiah lived. By this almost
casual allusion we learn that Jeremiah had at least one supporter,
besides Ezekiel, in the prophetic circle.

> *Reflection:* Truth has her heroes, less publicized than
> liars but more enduring, for "truth is the daughter of
> time."

Clearly, to describe Jeremiah as "lonely" does not mean
that he was friendless or entirely unsupported. But in that

internal struggle and sorrow which a wife or an equal might have shared, he remained a solitary man, enduring the loneliness of the excellent, the pioneer, the long-distance runner.

Jeremiah's Foes

When he was called, Jeremiah was warned to be prepared for opposition from "the kings of Judah, its princes, its priests, and the people of the land" (1:18); later, the "official" (royal) prophets were added to that list (2:26; 4:9; 32:32). His individual foes were spokesmen of hostile groups rather than personal enemies, and the reasons why such a man as Jeremiah — sincere, unselfseeking, patriotic — should be so persecuted require investigation.

Priests, of course, had personal interests vested in the hill shrines and in the temple, and naturally they resented Jeremiah's attack upon the existing forms of worship. His sermon in the temple (7:1–8:3; chap. 26), in which he criticized Judah's reliance upon ritual and warned that this most sacred shrine could itself become like rejected Shiloh, roused the priests' fury. In their sentencing of Jeremiah to death for this blasphemy, they were supported by prophets, the people, and most of the princes, but friendly princes intervened to save Jeremiah.

Undeterred, Jeremiah later castigated the priests' tolerance of pagan practices in the valley of Hinnom, having invited "senior priests" to witness his words, both in the valley and within the temple (19:1–20:6). The officer responsible for good order, Pashhur the priest, dealt to Jeremiah the punishment usual for brawlers in the sacred precincts: a harsh beating and a night in the public stocks.

The priests' opposition was not due entirely to self-interest. They were not mistaken in thinking that Jeremiah's actions were directed against their leadership of Judah, for he did not hesitate to accuse them of profaneness, falseness, and failure to inquire of the Lord (2:8; 6:13; 8:10; 23:11). So often the existing order in religion hinders the new demands of God when new dangers threaten and new situations call for larger visions of God.

Behind the opposition of the prophets lay a deep difference of understanding and a clash of authorities. The recognized prophets deeply resented Jeremiah's charges that they prophesied lies, dealing falsely with the people and their situation, prophesying by Baal, and offering vain hopes, folly, deceit, and peace when there was no peace (charges repeated some eighteen times).

Jeremiah did not question the value of prophecy. The prophets of old were God's servants, "persistently sent" by God (repeated five times). But not all who appeared were so "sent"; not all had "stood in God's council" before coming forth to announce his decrees. Of some prophets, Jeremiah declared their lives were "horrible," "evil"; he said they repeated each other's words, were "reckless," prophesied their own dreams, were "madmen"; they "anger God" (14:14; chap. 23; 27:15; etc.)

Commanded not to pray for Judah, Jeremiah pleaded as excuse for the people's waywardness the misleading instruction given by their prophets. God's reply was to repudiate their "lying vision," "worthless divination," and "deceit" (14:11-16).

In protest against an attempted conspiracy to revolt, Jeremiah walked about the streets wearing a wooden yoke symbolizing the yoke of Babylon that God had laid upon Judah. The "official" prophets replied that the tables would soon be turned, and one of them, Hananiah, declared that people already in exile would return within two years. Jeremiah reaffirmed his own message, and warned Hananiah of early death — a warning soon fulfilled (chaps. 27, 28). Even among the Jews already in Babylon prophets arose to contradict Jeremiah's predictions;

these, too, Jeremiah warned of divine punishment for grossly misleading God's people (chap. 29).

The underlying problem — that of deciding which among many contrary voices truly spoke for God — called for extended analysis and discussion, and in dealing fully with it Jeremiah showed that he counted it important (23:9-40). For the other prophets' opposition rested ultimately upon their very different viewpoint: they thought that the people were simply to be consoled and the royal authority upheld at all costs, whereas Jeremiah thought the people were to be prepared for tragedy and the royal policy was to be adjusted to realities. Behind this difference lay a different reading of future events: the other prophets declared that God would miraculously deliver his people, whereas Jeremiah declared that Babylon must certainly conquer demoralized Judah. Behind this lay a different view of God: the other prophets perceived him as one bound by covenant to be gracious to Israel however she behaved, whereas Jeremiah perceived him as one who was gracious to whom he chose to be gracious, but a God of judgment to those who deserved judgment.

Jeremiah's difficulties with the civic rulers arose from his being as concerned for the political fate of his people as for their religious condition. For him, faith and fate were interlocked. He accused the rulers of being themselves spiritually unprepared for the approaching crisis. The looming danger was the result of the faithlessness and the incompetence of "the shepherds," whose flock was therefore "led astray," "scattered"; "they have forgotten their fold" (23:1-14; 50:6).

Chief political responsibility lay, of course, with the kings. In early days, Jeremiah opposed attempts to rebel against Babylon as hopeless and perilous. Jehoiakim was wholly antagonistic to Jeremiah's moral and religious position; Zedekiah was too weak to restrain priests or princes. As the end drew nearer, Jeremiah's advice to surrender seemed to the authorities daily more dangerous, weakening the hands of the defenders; meanwhile, the first exile of leading citizens deprived Jeremiah of influential supporters.

Jeremiah seems to have trusted his evident patriotism and his grief for the city to disprove accusations of treason, but when he attempted to visit Anathoth during a lull in the final siege, he was arrested, charged with treason, and kept under arrest to the end. In the clash between the rulers' duty (as they saw it) to maintain the city's morale and his duty to warn of imminent defeat, Jeremiah could only wait to be vindicated by events.

Female Bit-Parts

At first reading, Jeremiah's drama appears to have an all-male cast. If that were true, it would not be characteristic, for Jeremiah shows real concern for the women misused and bereaved in those fateful days. He urges women to teach their daughters a lament, because the horrors of siege and defeat will fall heavily upon them. Four times he mentions the giving of wives to captors, and he warns the men that none shall be left to bury their wives and daughters. If women are not part of the main action, they are present, so to speak, in the wings.

But Jeremiah says something more, highlighting the strong influence of women in society, either for ill or for good. Early, in Jerusalem, and more boldly at the end, in Egypt, the women were active — defiantly so — in maintaining the pagan worship of the "queen of heaven," baking the votive sweetcakes and encouraging the children to gather kindling for the sacred fires. Jeremiah knew that the moral standard of any society never rises above that of its women. On the other hand, Huldah the prophetess also stood briefly off center stage but was influential for good in supporting Josiah's reform. Neither the gift of prophecy nor the quality of wisdom was a male preserve in ancient Judah. It seems a pity Jeremiah did not mention Huldah.

The one woman whom Jeremiah does name is still further offstage, but she is unforgettably introduced. She is Jacob's beloved Rachel, who "died, and . . . was buried on the way to Ephrath (that is, Bethlehem), and Jacob set up a pillar upon her grave; it is the pillar of Rachel's tomb, which is there to this day" — so records Genesis 35:19-20 (cf. Gen. 48:7).

With magnificent imagination, Jeremiah pictures the stricken exiles sadly leaving Jerusalem, and fancies he can hear, within that tomb as they pass, "a voice . . . in Ramah, lamentation and bitter weeping. Rachel is weeping for her children; she refuses to be comforted for her children, because they are not" (31:15). This is a fitting threnody upon the whole frustrating story of Israel, the painful ministry of Jeremiah, and the bleak tragedy of Judah. It is a lament well worthy of Matthew's skillful and poignant echoing long afterward, and again at Bethlehem (cf. Matt. 2:17-18).

5

Supporting a Good King

Josiah, at twenty-two, had been king for about fourteen years when Jeremiah was called to be a prophet, and for nearly eighteen years Jeremiah gave respect and approval to a ruler near his own age. The royal annals say that Josiah "did what was right in the eyes of the Lord, and walked in all the way of David his father." Jeremiah's tribute was spoken to Josiah's son: "Did not your father eat and drink [as one contented with enough?] and do justice and righteousness? . . . He judged the cause of the poor and needy; . . . Is not this to know me? says the Lord" (22:15-16).

The Chronicler mentions the reforming zeal that Josiah exhibited from the age of twenty, and the extended mourning of the people at his early death. Ben Sirach, about 180 B.C., recorded the "fragrance" of Josiah's memory, adding, "in the days of wicked men he strengthened godliness" (Sirach 49:1-3).

With such piety in high places, Jeremiah might have hoped for a sympathetic hearing. But Josiah was young, the memory of Manasseh was powerful, and the immature ardor of the new king was more tolerated than shared. The political situation was menacing. Jeremiah does not name the Scythians, but there is little doubt that these encroaching marauders provoked his earliest utterances.

1:13-19   For in addition to the sight of the almond tree in blossom, Jeremiah saw — apparently soon after — a boiling pot standing upon a fireplace open toward the north and fanned by a strong north wind. The details are obscure, but Ezekiel later elaborated the idea that Jerusalem was a pot needing to be boiled dry and burnt to cleanse the blood and filth within her: "this city is the cauldron, and we are the flesh" (Ezek. 24:3-14; 11:3; for "Scythians," see "Foreign Affairs" in Chapter 2).

So Jeremiah interpreted what he saw, a sign that "all the tribes of the kingdoms of the north" (v. 15) would bring evil upon the gates of Jerusalem and the cities of Judah. In this way, God would judge Judah for forsaking him for other gods, "the works of their own hands" (v. 16). In the face of this peril, Jeremiah was again urged to go wherever God would command and to speak fearlessly all that God would give him to say. For God would be with him.

> *Reflection:* An early almond tree, a boiling pot: God's call to service comes in diverse ways, and may be full of promise or of foreboding, an opportunity for self-fulfillment or an urgent need. Either way, obedience brings promise of divine enabling.

Before the Reform

Jeremiah's first task was to warn of imminent calamity and interpret it not as misfortune but as judgment. The suggestion that repentance could still avert the worst evils (4:14; 6:8) would have more appeal *before* Josiah's reformation than afterward, when the people would feel that repentance had been tried and had failed. The similarity of these early chapters to the message of Zephaniah also places them at the beginning of Jeremiah's ministry. They summarize some five years of public protest and warning when Jeremiah was young and inexperienced.

2:1–3:5 A single poem summarizes the message that Jeremiah was first commissioned to "go" (from Anathoth?) and "proclaim" at Jerusalem. It is addressed to all the families of the house of *Israel* because, since the fall of the northern kingdom, Judah alone represented the chosen nation. Josiah exercised considerable authority over such scattered people as remained as far as Samaria, Naphtali, and Megiddo, and Jeremiah's earliest fears and hopes likewise embraced both the remnant of northern Israel and Judah.

In language reminiscent of Hosea, the poem movingly recalls the nation's earlier days when Israel first "walked after" the Lord as a dutiful bride, protected by him. Wherein, Jeremiah asks, did God fail her, that she turned to worthless gods, defiling God's inheritance? Never had it been known, from Cyprus to Arabia, for even a heathen nation to change its gods. Yet Israel forsook her fountain of living (fresh) water for dry and broken cisterns. She turned for help to Egypt's Nile and Assyria's Euphrates, only to find them bitter (2:2-19; but verses 14-17, a lament over Josiah's death, are obviously intrusive; the passage makes better sense without them).

All Israel's apostasy has followed from her breaking God's yoke long ago, refusing obedience, and choosing the lewd worship and the Baals at the hill shrines. She is no longer God's "choice vine" but a wild plant bearing sour grapes, no longer his pure bride but obsessed with defiling passions. She races about lustfully like a wild animal in heat. A shameful and profitless apostasy it has proved, with a different god for every township. Yet the people blame God (2:20-29).

For all that, God had sought often to discipline them (3:3)

and to instruct them, although (under Manasseh) they had killed
his messengers. Why does Israel so foolishly assert her so-called
freedom and so unnaturally forget her God, her best adornment?
Now neither protestations of innocence nor political maneuver-
ings will save her. The people's present trust in Egypt will end in
humiliation, as did their former trust in Assyria. Such persistent
infidelity cannot be overlooked, nor the adulterous wife wel-
comed home again (contrast Hos. 3:1-3 and cf. Deut. 24:1-4).
Nor again will insincere, wheedling appeals to "my father" hide
guilt so deeply dyed (2:30–3:5). "This is how you talk, but you
do all the evil you can" (3:5, NIV).

> *Reflection:* Jeremiah's first message is forthright and
> stern. There are times when every godly life needs to
> hear things in these tones. All sentiment softens, but
> especially religious sentiment.

3:6–4:2 This prophecy is dated in Josiah's time; 3:18
reads like a later comment, perhaps added when these passages
were written down. The mixture of prose and poetry likewise
suggests later arrangement. Here we are reminded of Jeremiah's
upbringing on the border of comparatively empty northern
Israel. Surely Judah should have learned to fear God's judgments
from her "divorced" sister's tragic experience (3:6-10).

Israel had had no such dramatic warning before her eyes. She
was therefore less culpable, yet sorely punished. Might not at least
a remnant (v. 14) yet return, humbled and penitent, to find mercy?
Then new and better leaders will be given her, and a personal
knowledge of God will take the place of devotion to the lost and
lamented symbol, the Ark once treasured at Shiloh. So the nation
might yet be one again, centered in Jerusalem (vv. 11-18).

In this way God's original plan might even yet be fulfilled
(v. 19 echoes v. 4). But Israel has disappointed God, like a
faithless wife or wayward sons; she has begun at last to realize

her folly. An appeal to the "back-turning" people to "turn back" once again to God evokes moving words of penitence, but an interruption in prose suggests that the penitence is silenced by despair (vv. 24-25, RSV; the NIV continues in poetry, making v. 24 penitent, v. 25 despairing). But God again renews his appeal on three conditions, undertaking still a fulfillment of the ancient promise to Abraham (3:19–4:2; in 3:23 the NIV has "idolatrous commotion," meaning ecstatic worship; 3:24 refers to infant sacrifice).

> *Reflection:* This address is notably less stern, though without compromise. If Israel is genuinely repentant, she may yet be reunited with God and with her southern sister; in Scripture, reconciliation is always on *both* levels.

4:3-4 This treasured saying is timeless; only its position, as fitting appendix to the foregoing appeal, places it in Josiah's reign. If a united nation is ever to be re-established, then Judah too must "drive the coulter deep to plough the living man from sleep," must cleanse her corporate life of pestilential weeds, must wear again the badge of God's covenant upon her very heart. Otherwise, wrath and not promise will fill her future. (Verse 3 may have furnished Jesus with a seed thought for the parable of the sower.)

> *Reflection:* This brief note puts Jeremiah's essential message in a nutshell.

4:5-31 A young prophet's accusations might have little effect until rumors of the southward approach of Scythian raiders throw Judah and her neighbors into a panic. Jeremiah's rallying cry to villagers to seek cover in the cities could scarcely be more startling: "Raise the signal — To Zion!" (v. 6, NEB). Once again the "aristocracy" — king, officials, priests, prophets — will be astounded (vv. 5-9).

But Jeremiah recalls old promises that Jerusalem shall be unharmed, and feels the people have been deceived (v. 10; perhaps the promises of Isaiah [2 Kings 19:32-34] now falsely appealed to in different circumstances, or perhaps utterances of false prophets). God's reply likens the invaders to a gathering storm and to the hot, all-destroying sirocco from the desert, blowing not for winnowing but for blasting; neither one is predictable. But God appeals that Judah will repent and be delivered while there is still time. The raiders' steady approach is signaled from distant Dan, then from nearer Mount Ephraim, until the sounds of war begin to be heard in the city itself. Neighboring nations also should be warned. Jeremiah's anguish vies with his accusations of faithlessness and folly (vv. 10-22).

There follows a marvelous vision of the bare, scorched earth behind the savage plunderers (vv. 23-28; v. 23 echoes Gen. 1:2; v. 27 seems to be a later, relenting comment). At length, men forsake the towns for hiding places in the open fields; meanwhile, Jerusalem prepares for invasion as a harlot for her lovers, though in the event she will resemble instead a pregnant woman butchered (vv. 29-31; "lovers" recalls the lewd gods Judah worshiped, gods who now desert their followers).

> *Reflection:* The remarkable alternation in this prophecy — from dramatic alarm to pitying protest, from warning to appeal, from anguish to accusation, from poetic vision to plain statement of fact and bitter irony — vividly reveals a youthful prophet feeling deeply for his people yet determined to speak truly. No true spokesman of God can remain unmoved by his message or aloof from his hearers' plight.

5:1-31; 9:3-9 This long poem — woven around the thrice-repeated refrain " 'Should I not punish them for this?' declares the Lord. 'Should I not avenge myself on such a nation as this?' " (5:9, 29; 9:9, NIV), and beginning and ending with the same theme, the prevailing want of integrity — clearly sets forth God's justification for his judgments. Chapters 6, 7, and 8, which intervene, introduce other themes and situations, though certain *verbal* links may explain the present broken "arrangement."

The expected foes, the Scythians, use a hitherto unknown tongue. They are plunderers, not colonizers, whose skillful archery and strength are death-dealing. There is no mention of horses, chariots, shields, or armor such as the Assyrians or Egyptians would use. These raiders "devour" sons and daughters as they do vines, fig trees, and cities; they are as ravenous as lions, wolves, and leopards. The mention of the famous drought (5:24-25, as 3:3); the poem's position, and its concern with both Israel and Judah (5:11); the thought of "refining" (9:7; cf. 6:27-30) — all suggest that these passages belong together to an early date. An obvious intrusion in prose at 5:18-19 announcing exile and the veiled hope in verse 10 that accords ill with the refrain appear to be adjustments by hindsight when the poem was later written down.

The message begins with Judah's deserving all that is coming upon her. Like Sodom of old, Jerusalem cannot provide even one righteous man to be hostage for the rest, not one who acts justly, seeks truth, and swears honestly, as God requires. Instead, they are "rock hard" in obduracy. Nor is this true of the ignorant only: their leaders are no better. Like wayward oxen, breaking the yoke and wandering away, they render themselves prey to wild beasts. For a nation so given to defiling idolatry, only punishment remains. The Lord's own vineyard must be destroyed (5:1-10).

The root of such unfaithfulness is deep skepticism: "He [God] will do nothing; no evil will come upon us. . . . The prophets will become wind" (vv. 12-13). God, therefore, will make Jeremiah's words flame and the people firewood! *Why* this skepticism? *Why* has Judah no fear of the Lord? Do they imagine they can rebel against him who controls the raging seas? Are they unaware that in opposing the giver of rains and harvest they only impoverish themselves? (vv. 11-25).

Faithless toward God, they are faithless also toward each other, waylaying and trapping their neighbors, filling their houses with stolen goods, growing rich and sleek through wickedness. They pervert justice; they callously ignore the poor and needy. And the appealing outcome of this general social decay is that their prophets lie, their priests "go hand in hand with them" (v. 31, NEB), and the people could not care less. How can such a situation end, except in disaster — shall not God avenge himself on such a nation as this? (vv. 26-31).

No one can any longer trust another. Tongues are trained to lie, to mislead; sharp words become arrows aimed by trained archers. In such a society men do not succeed by holding fast to truth: "they are not valiant for truth" (v. 3, NIV). Friends, even brethren, beware of each other; each "Jacobs" (overreaches, supplants) his brother. All live in deception, at home amid lies, speaking cordially while planning harm. Should not God punish for this? Deepest evil of all, "'in their deceit they refuse to acknowledge me,' declares the Lord" (v. 6, NIV; 9:3-9).

> *Reflection:* The idea that God has a "duty" to punish sounds strange to modern ears, yet not to condemn is to condone. Besides, as with reconciliation, so with integrity: as we behave toward God, so in the end we behave toward our fellows.

6:1-26 Since chapter 7 certainly belongs to the reign of Jehoiakim, this passage, with its postscript (vv. 27-30), evidently closes the whole section concerning Jeremiah's ministry before Josiah's reform. It consists of five short poems divided by the refrain "This is what the Lord (Almighty) says" (NIV). This arrangement, the repeated reference to coming enemies "from the north" and the description of them, and some nine echoes of earlier poems confirm that these poems belong together and belong to Jeremiah's earlier years.

(i) **vv. 1-5:** Benjaminites who earlier took refuge in Jerusalem are now urged to flee southward, using Tekoa and Beth-haccherem as rallying points, because the city is no longer safe (cf. 4:5-6). With bitter irony, the fierce besiegers are likened to shepherds with their flocks grazing beyond the city walls! They are heard debating the best time for an unexpected assault. At first they say, "Let us attack at noon!" but the siesta delays it, so the cry becomes, "Let us attack by night!" Against this violent onslaught "out of the north," Jerusalem offers no more resistance than a "comely and delicately bred" maiden.

(ii) **vv. 6-8:** But it is the Lord who commands this, for punishment, since Jerusalem persists in wickedness, violence, and oppression, being sick at heart. In verse 6 the city appears doomed, but in verse 8 there appears to be some hope; perhaps verse 8 reflects later hindsight, because the city was not destroyed at this time. (In v. 7, the RSV's "a well keeps its water *fresh*" [emphasis mine] is more factual than the NIV's "a well pours out its water.")

(iii) **vv. 9-15:** God orders a thorough gleaning of his vine, Judah, as the grape-gatherer "passes his hand" along it the second time, backward up the stem, to find the last grape. The prophet asks whom he is to warn, since the people will not hear or value God's word. He can barely restrain the righteous anger that this evokes in him, and he is told to pour it out upon all, of each age and both sexes, from least to greatest. Prophets and priests especially are lying comforters, content with superficial changes (Josiah's earliest efforts at reform?) when radical

change is needed. Therefore *all* shall surely share punishment.

(iv) vv. 16-21: Previous warnings have been spurned: Judah has refused her earlier instruction in the ways that lead to rest, ignored the trumpets of God's watchmen warning of danger. Let surrounding nations therefore understand why Jerusalem is punished. Elaborate and costly worship remains unacceptable if God's law is not obeyed. God himself will make the people of Judah stumble; since they refuse to walk in his ways, he will bring about their fall. (In v. 18 the RSV has "congregation"; the NIV has "witnesses," apparently implying "spectators." The NIV makes v. 21 a separate fragment, despite its echo of v. 16.)

(v) vv. 22-26: A further vivid description of the Scythians, and the panic and peril they will bring as the scourge of God, summarizes the whole section. Horses are mentioned this time, but the primitive bow and spear are still the only weapons mentioned; cruelty and terror rather than conquest and rule are the Scythians' aim. They come not in regular battle formation, as a disciplined army, but "like" such (NIV). The very rumor of them breeds panic; the roads are unsafe, women lament as though already bereaved, "terror is on every side," for "suddenly the destroyer will come upon us" (cf. 50:41-43, an attack upon Babylon).

Reflection: Inevitably there comes to all a time when warnings cease, harvests have to be reaped, doors close, opportunities pass by, debts fall due, and we find ourselves what we have made ourselves. It is called "living in a moral universe," God's world.

6:27-30 These verses serve as a postscript not only to five short poems but also to this period of Jeremiah's ministry.

As the enemy draws near ("the bellows blow fiercely"), God himself reviews Jeremiah's work. By description, accusation, warning, and appeal, Jeremiah has been "assaying and refining" God's precious ore, his people. To no avail. Stubbornness, rebellion, and hardness have resisted purifying; the wicked are not removed. "Refuse silver are they called, for the Lord has rejected them" (v. 30): that solemn verdict closes in foreboding and defeat Jeremiah's first attempt at prophesying.

Prophecies of Less Certain Date

What else Jeremiah may have said or done during his first years we cannot know for certain. Other passages, now appearing later in Jeremiah's "collected works," may date from his early ministry; a few most probably do; but clear clues are rare. We can only weigh possibilities, taking care not to distort meaning to fit theory.

13:1-11 Jeremiah is bidden to buy and wear a new sash (of priestly linen?), then to hide it in a damp, rocky crevice, and later to retrieve it, "spoiled" and good for nothing. God explains this as a warning that he will "spoil" the pride of Judah for refusing his word and seeking other gods, although he had bound this people to himself as closely as an ornamental (priestly?) sash. Such dramatic actions by a prophet would set the whole city to speculating on his meaning.

Such is the essence of the prophecy (vv. 9-11), shorn of attendant difficulties. Chief of these are *where* the sash is to be hidden and what that implies. The AV (KJV), RV, and RSV say "by the Euphrates"; the NIV and NEB have "at/by Perath," the NIV having a footnote saying "possibly the Euphrates." Jeremiah wrote (or dictated) "Perath," which has been explained as either a form of Parah, a town in Benjamin near Anathoth (Josh. 18:23), or the regular word for (the) River, which the Greek version, followed by older English versions, understood as Euphrates.

Because of that last translation, Jeremiah's action has usually been interpreted as a prophetic symbol of the coming exile in Babylon. If that interpretation is true, the passage belongs, far more probably, to the reign of Jehoiakim or later. But then difficulties multiply. The Euphrates was four hundred miles away, Babylon six hundred, a round-trip of eight or twelve hundred miles each time. Who then in Judah would know where Jeremiah had gone, or why? Jeremiah could have told them, but he could have done that without traveling: either way the dramatic impression would be lost. Some make the whole incident a vision — to which the same objection applies. In any case, Judah did not *return* from Babylon "spoiled" and good for nothing: she was exiled there because she was already so — the sash should have been "spoiled" from the start. The Exile was to cure, not cause, her corruption.

By retaining the original word "Perath," modern translations suggest that the sash was hidden someplace in Palestine, where Jeremiah's visits and actions would be reported and discussed. This could be Parah, near Jeremiah's home, or *possibly* (E)phratah (Bethlehem), or more probably any crevice by a "perath," a river, where the linen would rot. If this is so, then no reference to Babylon or to exile was intended; the meaning is precisely as given in verses 9-11: something once honored and close to God is now stained, "spoiled," and rendered useless to him.

That interpretation makes the whole passage parallel in thought to other earlier passages that speak of the once-loved bride, now adulterous, the people redeemed to inherit Canaan but now defiling it, the cherished son who proved faithless (2:2, 5-8; 3:1, 19-20). And those thoughts belong to Jeremiah's earliest ministry.

Reflection: Privilege enhances responsibility. Amos had said, "You only have I known . . . ; therefore I will punish you" (Amos 3:2). Jesus was to say, "To whom much is given, of him will much be required" (Luke 12:48).

14:1–15:9   We know of no such prolonged drought in Jeremiah's later years to evoke this message. But in 3:3 and 5:24-25, allusions occur to a withholding of rain in the earlier years; in 15:4 the memory of Manasseh's reign is still fresh. Moreover, 14:3 echoes 2:13, 14:10 echoes 2:36, and 14:13 recalls 4:10: Jeremiah was certainly thinking in these terms in his earlier years.

Following a vivid description of the drought's effects (14:1-6; in v. 4, the RSV describes the ground as "dismayed"; the NIV has "cracked"), Jeremiah pleads eloquently that in this crisis God will act for Judah, not hold himself aloof like a passing stranger or one too confused to help. God's reply is that the people of Israel have persistently wandered from him and must be punished. Jeremiah therefore is not to pray for them (vv. 7-12).

But Jeremiah argues that the common people are misled by their optimistic prophets. God repudiates such men, threatening them with famine and sword. A moving poetic lament follows, leading to renewed pleading: has God then utterly rejected Judah? As priest, Jeremiah acknowledges on Judah's behalf the people's persistent sinfulness, but pleads for them on the basis of God's ancient covenant with Israel, and boldly asks, "Are there any among the false gods of the nations that can bring rain? Or can the heavens give showers?" Only God *can* help! (vv. 13-22; in v. 18 the RSV says prophets and priests "ply their trade through the land"; the NEB has "go begging").

Again God answers sternly, declaring that even Moses and

Samuel, famed intercessors, could not now alter his mind
toward Judah. The people are to be dismissed to the punishments prepared for them. God's own lament follows, recalling
the sorrows he has heaped upon Jerusalem without evoking
response. "I am weary of relenting" (15:1-9; in v. 2, "captivity"
gains meaning from the fate of northern Israel).

> *Reflection:* This is a most solemn reminder that there
> are situations and states of soul for which prayer itself
> is no cure. See 1 John 5:16.

17:5-8 This exquisite poem bears no clear evidence of
date and has no connection with its present context, but its
main lesson, the contrast in experience between those who trust
in man and those who trust in God, echoes 2:14-19 (cf. Isa.
31:2), and verse 8 makes yet another allusion to drought. These
suggest an early date, while the hope that Judah might flourish
if she returns to faith likewise fits Jeremiah's early ministry
better than his later, more pessimistic days.

The poem's meaning, like its beauty, is obvious. If it
provided inspiration for Psalm 1, it is interesting that Jeremiah
contrasts faith and non-faith, whereas the Psalmist, in similar
terms, contrasts those who delight in God's law with those who
do not.

> *Reflection:* Jeremiah has "reflected" to some purpose!

17:19-27 Jeremiah is commanded to stand at each gate
of Jerusalem in turn, beginning at that traditionally used by
royalty, and forbid all trading and associated work on the Sabbath. If Judah will heed, then Davidic kings will yet enter, and
"this city shall be inhabited for ever" (v. 25). Abundant offerings shall then replace the goods of trade. If Judah will not
heed, then the gates and the city shall be destroyed by fire.

Many have felt this passage to be wholly unlike Jeremiah.

It makes Judah's future depend upon her keeping one external commandment. It belongs more to the post-exilic emphasis upon everything distinctively Jewish than to the inward, personal religion of Jeremiah. It closely resembles the attitude of Ezra and Nehemiah (especially Neh. 13:15-22), though why a post-exilic story should appear among the memoirs of Jeremiah is not explained.

But this whole argument is unconvincing. Jeremiah's inward, personal piety by no means *excluded* all outward, corporate expressions of worship and obedience, any more than the personal, inward faith of Jesus excluded synagogue services or Sabbath reverence. Like Amos (Amos 8:5), Jeremiah would treasure the very ancient Sabbath rule not for merely ritual, ceremonial reasons but for pious, traditional, humanitarian reasons, as Deuteronomy enjoins. In emphasizing obedience to the divine covenant, Jeremiah must sometimes have suggested clear instances of such obedience, among which the requirement of Sabbath observance certainly figured, acknowledging God's authority over the people's time and their business life. The Sabbath recalled God's sovereignty in creation, gave opportunity for worship, and afforded rest for the laboring people, each point congenial to Jeremiah.

It is significant, too, that Jeremiah did not (like Nehemiah) demand that the city gates be closed for the Sabbath or that loiterers outside be punished. It seems probable that Nehemiah acted upon Jeremiah's precedent but in post-exilic zeal went further in demand and threat.

If then we accept the passage as Jeremiah's, the conditional promise that the monarchy shall remain and the city stand *for ever* can hardly belong to the later years, when Jeremiah was certain that the throne was doomed and the city would be destroyed. The promise of abundant offerings, too, reflects the prophet's earlier priestly attitude toward sacrifices rather than his later doubts. The promise is in fact the converse of the early warning that without obedience, costly ceremonial acts are futile (see 6:19-20).

The notion of a regular and recurring "holy day" (or "day of ill omen") for the cessation of labor is widespread and very ancient. The Mosaic law itself, in rehearsing the obligations of the divine covenant, bids Israel *"remember* the Sabbath day," tracing its origin to the creation story. In selecting this one specific and measurable example of public obedience to God's laws, Jeremiah chooses the one with the greatest authority and antiquity, and one wholly unrelated to the forms of worship at shrine and temple that he so deeply suspects.

> *Reflection:* Generalized and abstract acknowledgment of "spiritual values" signifies nothing if we never in literal fact do anything that God plainly commands. "Why do you call me 'Lord, Lord,' and not do what I tell you?" asked Jesus (Luke 6:46).

18:1-17 The story of Jeremiah's visit to the potter is probably the best known of all these reminiscences of the prophet, and its apparent assurance that God's grace can remold the most misshapen of us to better use and beauty is always welcome. That insight is, most thankfully, entirely true, and illustration for it may be extracted from this story. But it is not Jeremiah's meaning.

Jeremiah is emphasizing that God is sovereign over individuals and nations, even as the potter has complete mastery over his clay. God has the fullest right to deal with people and nations as he chooses, even to change his mind and revise his declared purpose concerning them in the light of their response to him: *"I will repent* of the evil that I intended. . . . *I will repent* of the good which I had intended" (vv. 7-10, emphasis mine). That is the essence of the message, and in that ancient world it had very far-reaching significance. *God is not bound,* not even by his own warnings and promises, *nor by his covenant with Israel* if Israel's disobedience changes the situation God planned.

This "freedom of God" is a central theme of Hebrew prophecy. Neighboring nations thought of their gods as indissolubly allied to them, both as localized in the national territory and as the transcendental ancestors of the nation, tribe, or clan. They were therefore bound to their people's defense and welfare, however the people behaved. Part of the attraction of the Canaanite cults for Israel was the assurance they gave that the gods of the soil, of the herd, of fertility, and of victory *had* to serve their people. But the essence of the covenantal relation to God, which stood at the heart of Hebrew religion from Moses onward and which the prophets recovered and emphasized, was that God's favor depended upon the people's obedience.

God himself in his goodness first delivered this people from Egypt; God set the terms of the covenant and offered his promises. But the people had to agree voluntarily, and God could fulfill his promises or withhold his favor as the people deserved. Israel's relationship with her God was thus unique, neither natural nor indissoluble but moral and conditional: "Listen to my voice, and do all that I command you. So shall you be my people, and I will be your God, that I may perform the oath which I swore to your fathers" (11:4-5) is the very essence of Jeremiah's theology.

And the story of the potter's freedom to adjust his purpose for his clay, according to its pliability under his hands, dramatically illustrates that truth. So Ezekiel, Jeremiah's disciple, expounded the same principle in detail (Ezek. 18:21-28, and again at 33:12-20). And so Paul argues vehemently the right of the potter over the clay, to make of it what he will (Rom. 9:19-21). Jeremiah's generation needed especially to learn this truth. At every warning they took refuge in the belief that God had undertaken to care for Israel and could not break his covenant. This confidence the false prophets fostered by assuring that no evil could ever befall *God's* people; with God on their side, all must be "peace, peace" (4:10; 5:12; 6:14). Jeremiah's figure of the supreme potter directly contradicted this false assumption.

But Jeremiah leaves open the possibility that disaster can still be avoided if the people return and amend their ways. This places the incident in Jeremiah's earlier ministry, and echoes of his early thoughts confirm this (cf. vv. 8-9 with 1:10; v. 13 with 2:10-11; v. 17 with 2:27 and 4:11). The people obdurately oppose their purposes to God's (v. 12), and the story closes with an invitation to neighboring nations to testify if such a thing has ever happened before, if any people has unnaturally and deliberately forgotten their god (vv. 13-17).

> *Reflection:* It is a salutary lesson, at any time, *never* to presume upon the faithfulness of God by claiming his promises while denying his claims; God is sovereign, not slave, of his people.

22:1-9 Every verse here, except verses 6-7, repeats something from Jeremiah's early preaching to form the introduction to a series of utterances on the kings of Judah. The emphasis on social justice is obviously appropriate. The new poetic fragment (vv. 6-7) almost defeats translation, as a comparison of modern versions will show. But the general purpose is clear: to describe the desolation of the royal line, the land, and the city. Neighboring peoples in wonder will ask "Why?" to which Jeremiah will answer once more, "Because they forsook the covenant of the Lord their God" (v. 9). That is why the beloved and beautiful woodland, like cedar-crowned Lebanon or the highlands of Gilead, will be laid waste by an army of destructive woodsmen.

> *Reflection:* Whatever a great tradition or high self-confidence or treasured promises might suggest, it is social righteousness alone that can exalt or preserve a city, a land, or a ruling house.

21:11-14 This passage is likewise very difficult to translate, to date, or to interpret. It seems clear that Jerusalem is here again warned of destruction as the consequence of social injustice, and "in the morning" (regular Hebrew for "as early as possible, promptly") shows that punishment follows soon (v. 12).

Despite uncertainties, the general impression of Jeremiah's early ministry under Josiah is consistent and clear, as we should expect if it rests *ultimately* on Baruch's record of Jeremiah's own account. The prophet was deeply moved by the unfaithfulness of Judah to the divine covenant upon which her welfare and destiny depended. That unfaithfulness was manifest in her idolatry, immorality, social injustice, and corrupted religious rites and thought. Jeremiah warned that God was as free to repudiate the covenant as Judah claimed to be.

In these first years, Jeremiah clung to the hope that Judah might avert disaster by repentance and amendment of her ways. His prediction of the approach of the Scythians proved untrue; they apparently passed Judah by on the way south toward Egypt. Nevertheless, Jeremiah knew the danger was only postponed, and the prophecy would be fulfilled — as events proved, by a still more deadly foe. The divine verdict stood: "Refuse silver they are called, for the Lord has rejected them. . . . Do not pray for the welfare of this people" (6:30; 14:11). Utterly faithful to his message, young Jeremiah yet found no pleasure in his task. But he had some important lessons still to learn.

Josiah's Reform — and After

One such lesson came soon, and sharply. When, in pursuit of his youthful purges of alien cults and his repair of the temple, Josiah was confronted with the rediscovered law-book and set about more radical reforms, Jeremiah must have felt that Judah's repentance and amendment had begun. His attitude to the reform movement has been much discussed, but it is difficult to believe that he did not sympathize fully with the king's intention. The removal of the hill shrines with their gross temptations, the centralization of worship where it could be officially overseen, the reconsecration of the nation to its ancient covenant with God, the supremacy of the prophetic outlook that seemed imminent — all were congenial to Jeremiah's thinking.

It is surprising, therefore, that Jeremiah never explicitly mentions Josiah's reforming initiative, even in his tribute to the king. Nor does the story of the reform in 2 Kings 23 mention Jeremiah. Some think that Jeremiah was silent from the date of the reform to the king's death, either because the reform left him nothing to add, or because he could not support and would not oppose a well-intentioned movement. This assumes he could not approve the more violent methods sometimes used (2 Kings 23:20 mentions the assassination of "heretical" priests) or the emphasis upon temple worship and animal sacrifice, as at the great Passover.

Jeremiah's whole emphasis, we are told again, was upon inward piety. His sermon in the temple (chaps. 7, 26) was a scathing indictment of reliance upon ritual worship and sacred places; 7:21-22 follows Amos and Hosea in denying that sacrifices were ever originally required by God. Jeremiah would have abolished the sacrificial system, not reformed it. As for the newfound law-book, Jeremiah appears to dismiss it as forgery in these famous words: "How can you say, 'We are wise, and the law of the Lord is with us?' But behold, the false pen of the scribes has made it into a lie" (8:8).

These arguments are of varying weight. As we have seen, there is no ground for supposing that Jeremiah's "inward piety" descended to a private and individualistic pietism with no formal or public expression at all. Nor can we imagine that the young priest-prophet set out from the start to abolish sacrificial

worship. If the newly discovered law-book was any version of
the book of Deuteronomy, it would not support such an attempt: Deuteronomy assumes the practice and insists upon its
worthy observance. That could have been Jeremiah's initial
attitude also. Further, careful reading of 8:8 shows that
Jeremiah does not challenge the authorship of the law-book but
asserts that *copyists* have, by their versions and comments, mis-
read, misinterpreted, and perhaps deliberately altered its meaning and application.

Almost certainly, the explanation of Jeremiah's silence
about Josiah's reform movement lies in the passage of time and
in disappointed hindsight. Forty years of public ministry is
long enough for any man as perceptive and honest as Jeremiah
to change his mind about many things; and even earlier, when
Baruch made his record, the reform was known to have failed.
If we free our minds of the assumption that any passage which
sounds "Deuteronomic" must be post-reformation, one passage
alone should convince us that Jeremiah at first fully supported
Josiah's attempted improvements.

11:1-23 Jeremiah is commanded to hear for himself the
words of "this covenant" (the phrase assumes it is already known
and is being discussed). He is then commanded to warn
Jerusalem of the curses that will fall upon disobedience; verse
3 refers to curses listed in Deuteronomy 27:15-26, to which
the people were instructed to answer "Amen." Jeremiah himself
now makes that required response (v. 5, NIV; v. 4 quotes
Deuteronomy 4:20; v. 5 refers also to Deuteronomy 7:12 and
11:9; there is no doubt that the newly discovered law-book is
in mind).

Jeremiah is next instructed to "proclaim" this covenant
in the streets of Jerusalem and in the cities of Judah (v. 6), as
the original basis of Israel's relationship with God. Such a
countrywide campaign promoting the covenant is approval
energetically expressed! But solemnly, too, for Jeremiah re-

minds Judah of the earlier proclamation at the Exodus, and the stubborn disobedience with which their fathers flouted it, with evil consequences (vv. 1-8).

In verses 9-17 the tone changes. The outcome of this campaign for the covenant is described with sternness, then with judgment. Not all the common people, in districts beyond reach of royal displeasure, would welcome the king's order to destroy the hill shrines and to worship only God and only at Jerusalem. Opposition would necessarily be secret: "revolt" in verse 9 of the RSV is more accurately "conspiracy," as the NIV has it. Even those who obeyed soon "turned back" (v. 10) to their former ways.

Thus the campaign was but fitfully and temporarily successful. The following years saw it almost forgotten, the reforming fit passed, and by the next reign former habits had been re-established. In the description of Judah, as Baruch then wrote it, may be found no less than twelve echoes of descriptions uttered before the reform. Prayer is again futile; God has pronounced evil against his "olive tree" to destroy it, tree and fruit together.

In verses 18-23 Jeremiah records his painful experience of "proclaiming the covenant" at Anathoth. Doubtless enraged by Jeremiah's support for reforms that would destroy his hometown's shrine and with it the status of his own kin, the men of Anathoth devised schemes to destroy him, "the tree with its fruit" (v. 19), if he persisted in prophesying. Even his brothers joined the plot. But God forewarned him. We can still feel the bitter disappointment in the vindictive prayer and pronouncement that burst from Jeremiah's heart (vv. 20-23; see 12:6).

This story of Anathoth's reaction, like Jeremiah's long friendship with the family of Shaphan (leaders in the reform movement; 2 Kings 22:12-14), confirms his initial enthusiasm for the reform movement, as the harshness of 11:9-17, 21-23 reveals his deep disappointment. In the end the reform lasted only about twelve years. With the death of Josiah at Megiddo, if not before, the impetus for it ceased and reaction set in. Jeremiah apparently fell silent for the closing years of Josiah's reign, watching Judah's renewed decline and losing hope. In his eulogy of Josiah he is silent about the abortive reform (22:15-16).

2:14-17   These verses express Jeremiah's feeling at this severe reverse. Is Israel a mere slave, to be so treated, a prey to others' violence, the "crown of [her] head" (Josiah) "broken" by men of Egypt? Why should this happen? Jeremiah has to reply, "Have you not [Judah and Josiah] brought this upon yourself?" For Josiah need not have meddled with Pharaoh Neco's northward push to assist Assyria. The event, in Jeremiah's eyes, was needless tragedy.

Assessment

Jeremiah's support of good king Josiah can scarcely be counted "successful." True, he presented with eloquence his analysis of Judah's spiritual condition, recalling the nation to its origin in the early "love" between God and Israel. He faithfully re-emphasized Israel's covenantal relationship with God and its implication for the ordering of the nation's life — the close connection of character and welfare. To him, God was righteous, and therefore life was basically moral: "I the Lord search the heart and examine the mind, to reward a man according to his conduct, according to what his deeds deserve" (17:10, NIV).

All this Jeremiah faithfully taught, courting no popularity, concealing no truth, fearing no opposition, seeking no reward. Yet his warnings fell on stubborn hearts, and his support of the king's efforts came to nothing. We know from numerous soliloquies and confessions that Jeremiah experienced private doubts and strong misgivings, feeling publicly discredited and inwardly "let down" by the God who had called him. To the people he loved his complaint after twenty-three years was simply "You have not listened. You have neither listened nor inclined your ears to hear" (25:3-4, 7).

Despite everything, Jeremiah was essentially right in his analysis, his prevision of events, and his understanding of God. The outcome of the most faithful ministry is always limited by the capacity and the response of those who receive it. Although Jeremiah's predictions about the approach of the Scythians were mistaken in detail, he was right about the growing danger to Judah from the north, now that Assyria was declining. The religious man's insight is often true even when his information is incomplete or inaccurate.

And Jeremiah was learning. First, that religious reform cannot possibly be imposed upon a people by royal decree, or even by some religious "authority." Second, that the laws of God cannot be imposed upon unwilling hearts simply upon the external authority of a book in the hands of scribes and priests. He came eventually to see that God's will must be discerned from within, "written on the heart," before it will win obedience. Third, Jeremiah was learning that neither eloquence nor argument, poetry nor appeal, suffice to teach some truths, but only hard experience and bitter regret — for example, the truth that the political identity of the Jewish state might have to be destroyed in order that the message of Jewry for the world might be preserved.

He was learning the high cost of faithful service to God in difficult days. The sharp disappointments of these early years undoubtedly deepened the prophet's understanding of God, fashioned his maturity, and in time engendered greatness.

6

Opposing a Bad King

A t Josiah's death, Judah appointed his twenty-three-year-old son, Jehoahaz, to the throne, perhaps discerning in him (as did the author of 2 Kings 23:31-32) tendencies that promised relaxation of reforming strictures. But Pharaoh Neco needed a docile ally, and within three months he enthroned one of Josiah's other sons, who was twenty-five, naming him Jehoiakim, and deported Jehoahaz to Egypt. Jeremiah broke his silence to make a brief comment:

22:10-12 Unlike the author of 2 Kings, Jeremiah showed intense pity for a man ("Shallum" = Jehoahaz; see 1 Chron. 3:15) given no time to reveal his individual character. But if he hoped that in time Jehoahaz would emulate his father, he was further disappointed. The people were still lamenting Josiah, but Jeremiah felt that Jehoahaz needed greater sympathy, exiled in a land Jeremiah would not name, never to return. Why Jeremiah published this four-line dirge at this time is not clear; its air of finality may have been intended to mark the end of an era. All was certainly changed thereafter, and Jeremiah faced a very different kind of king.

With Jehoiakim's accession, reform was finally abandoned. Frustration and resentment over the sudden death of Josiah may have clouded the faith and discouraged the zeal of the reform party. Jehoiakim preferred Manasseh's example, and under his influence the old pagan cults again became dominant. The reign began under poor auspices, the people preferring Jehoahaz and Egypt exacting heavy taxation (2 Kings 23:35). Yet Jehoiakim built extravagantly, by forced labor, bribery, and violent exactions. Jeremiah's judgment of Jehoiakim is severe.

22:13-23; 36:30-31 With Jehoiakim's extravagance and oppression Jeremiah contrasts Josiah's simpler life-style and his treatment of his people as brethren, not slaves. "Is ostentation the hallmark of kingship?" he asks in effect. The charge of "shedding innocent blood" probably refers to the king's murder of Uriah and the attempts on Jeremiah's life. Such a king shall die unlamented and receive the burial of an ass, being dragged outside the city gates and thrown down to rot, a fate which would carry disgrace even to Sheol. He shall have no royal successor, Jeremiah declares, and his prophecy was fulfilled: Jehoiakim's son reigned for only three months.

Judah is urged to lament, on the bare eastern hills for wider proclamation, that her foreign allies have been "crushed," failing her as badly as her own rulers have done. As for her present ruler, luxuriating in his palace (22:23; the NIV cites 1 Kings 7:2) — how he will groan when his time comes! Jeremiah's verdict upon Jehoiakim is as courageous as it is damning. 36:30-31 clearly echoes it.

17:9-13 These lines probably contain Jeremiah's fragmentary reflections upon Jehoiakim's death at age thirty-six, "in the midst of his days" (v. 11). Certainly Jehoiakim's heart was devious enough to serve Egypt or Babylon as the occasion required. But God rewards a man's ways with justice. The partridge proverb (probably folklore) is apposite: her borrowed brood leave their alien parent as soon as possible, as ill-gotten gains fall from oppressive hands. The verses breathe a sense of divine justice having fallen upon an evil reign, a quiet exultation at the removal from power of one who forsook God, and a renewed trust in "the hope of Israel" for better days to come.

The story that earned these condemnations is easily summarized, though Jehoiakim's eleven years of rule were extremely active ones for Jeremiah:

- *First Period:* This was "the beginning of his reign," from 608-605 B.C. As Egypt's vassal, Jehoiakim was paying heavy tribute.
- *Second Period:* This period ran from the crucial battle of Carchemish in 605 B.C. to 602/1 B.C. Egypt being defeated, Jehoiakim became a nominal vassal and tributary to Babylon, but enjoyed comparative freedom while Nebuchadrezzar was preoccupied elsewhere. At this time Jeremiah's attention is divided between foreign and domestic affairs.
- *Third Period:* This was the span from 602/1 to 597 B.C. With Nebuchadrezzar turning his attention to Palestine, Jehoiakim became fully subject to Babylon. In 598 B.C. he attempted rebellion. Again preoccupied elsewhere, Nebuchadrezzar employed local garrisons to harass Judah. When Nebuchadrezzar returned to Jerusalem, Jehoiakim had died.

First Period

The ruling party in the state was now hostile to all that Jeremiah stood for, and the king a personal enemy. Disappointed, for some time silent, but still indomitable, Jeremiah set himself to salvage what remained of Judah's religion, and so to prepare for what must lie beyond the inevitable catastrophe.

7:1–8:3; 26:1-24 Sometime early in the new reign,
Jeremiah appeared at the gate of the temple to preach a sermon
that immediately imperiled his life. We have two accounts of
the incident (cf. 7:12 and 26:6, 9), one concentrating on
Jeremiah's message, the other on its consequences. The sermon
was prolonged — "So you shall speak all these words to them"
(7:27; cf. 26:2, 8, 12, 15). Two themes enraged priests, prophets, and people: Jeremiah's disparagement of the temple and
his warning that Jerusalem would be destroyed (7:1–8:3).

"All the cities of Judah" had gathered for prayer and
sacrificing, apparently in view of some crisis involving Judah's
permanently "dwelling in this place" and needing the help of
"the Lord of hosts" (7:3; "Lord Almighty," NIV). Although
Josiah's reform had sought to centralize worship at the temple,
Jeremiah now vigorously attacked the slogan "The temple of
the Lord, the temple of the Lord, the temple of the Lord" (7:4;
meaning probably "the temple of the Lord — that's the
thing!"), and the deceptive, essentially superstitious attitude
that lay behind it. For the temple was being used not for grateful
worship and the renewal of covenantal vows but as a "den of
robbers" (7:11), giving refuge to people who oppressed the
defenseless, murdered the innocent, practiced idolatry and adultery, stole, perjured themselves, and defiled the holy place with
their abominations (7:1-11).

These "worshipers" supposed that merely by presenting
themselves in the temple they could claim divine forgiveness
(7:10). Jeremiah insisted that unless their worship was accompanied by radical moral reform, God would do to the Jerusalem
temple what he had done to the temple at Shiloh. The shadow of
that ruin had lain in Jeremiah's mind since boyhood (7:12-15).

Nor would God hear prayer for these people. In their
revived "family fiesta" acknowledging the queen of heaven, they
invoked only their own utter confusion. Prayer for such people
is out of place (7:16-20).

As for their multiplied sacrifices, from soiled hands burnt offerings consumed on the altar are no different from "butcher's meat" intended for human consumption. To this scathing comment Jeremiah added that when Israel left Egypt, God had demanded not burnt offerings and sacrifices but obedience to his covenant conditions (7:21-26). So at Sinai the sacrificial blood sprinkled on altar and people had pledged God and Israel to each other, to bless and to obey respectively. But as from the first the fathers had withheld their obedience, so Judah still maintained the ritual while refusing to obey, thus rendering her sacrifices meaningless and hypocritical (7:24-26).

This axiom of Hebrew prophecy — that moral obedience is "better," more important, than animal sacrifices — was bound eventually to displace animal sacrifice entirely (see 1 Sam. 15:22-23; Hos. 6:6; Isa. 1:11-15; Mic. 6:6-8; and Pss. 40:6; 51:16). For Jeremiah himself, animal sacrifice was part of the inherited pattern of worship, and better rules for its observance were part of Josiah's reformation. After the failure of that reformation, however, Jeremiah saw that the sacrificial ritual had become a substitute for obedience, and he then declared that originally God had not commanded burnt offerings and sacrifices at all (7:22). So far had his mind moved, and so wide had the gulf between him and the religious establishment become.

Jeremiah says that God had forewarned him that his message would not be heard. Obedience, discipline, integrity — all have died, and only funeral lamentation is appropriate. Judah has practiced "unthinkable" abominations, even within the temple: Ezekiel includes Tammuz worship, sun worship, and Egyptian animal worship among them (Ezek. 8:7-17). In addition, Judah has rebuilt the countryside high places for cultic worship, among them Topheth (a term of execration) in the valley of ben Hinnom, where infant sacrifice was again practiced (7:27-31).

In consequence (see 7:32–8:3), temple and city would be

destroyed, the living would endure a living death and the dead lie unburied (following a great battle?). The bones of the long dead, their tombs plundered, would lie exposed to the heavenly bodies they had stupidly worshiped, and "death shall be preferred to life by all the remnant that remains of this evil family" (8:3).

It is scarcely surprising that Jeremiah's congregation resented a sermon so insulting and frightening. "The priests and the prophets and all the people" laid hold of him, saying, "You shall die!" (26:1-9). Some of the princes arranged a trial, at which Jeremiah defended himself with dignity, supported by certain of the princes and people who recalled good king Hezekiah's reverent response to Micah's similar warnings. So Jeremiah escaped, though the fate of Uriah shows it was no imaginary peril; ministry under Jehoiakim had begun with a menacing confrontation (26:10-24).

> *Reflection:* This surely was the point at which a weaker man, so disillusioned, so threatened, would have given up. But God's servants "need to persevere so that when [they] have *done the will of God,* [they] will receive what he has promised" (Heb. 10:36, NIV; emphasis mine).

8:4–9:2, 10 (9:3-9 belongs to 5:1-31.) Position links this passage with 26:1, but the change to poetry suggests a different situation. It appeared that the king's allegiance to Egypt might need adroit adjustment because prince Nebuchadrezzar was threatening Palestine's frontiers.

Judah's persistent waywardness is contrary to all that is natural in intelligent creatures; she plunges headlong into sin like a battle-crazed horse. Her leaders claim to be wise in the requirements of God, but the written laws they appeal to have misled them, and they constantly refuse the deeper wisdom of *obeying* what they claim to know (8:4-9).

The surprising charge that the written law of God could

mislead (v. 8) reveals a third major shift in Jeremiah's position equal to those concerning temple worship and animal sacrifice. He had once supported the reformation based upon a written law-book; now he has learned that a religious movement dependent upon a book is vulnerable to misquotation and misinterpretation. To use but one example: "The first-born of your sons you shall give to me" (Exod. 22:29) might well be understood to require infant sacrifice (see Mic. 6:7).

As a priest, Jeremiah certainly knew and valued the sacred writings of his people. Later, Baruch's record of Jeremiah's messages marks one step toward translating living prophecy into Scripture (chap. 36; cf. 30:2; 51:60). But while documentation could preserve for all times truths revealed at particular times and places, it could also be liable to manipulation and even become a substitute for the living voice of God speaking in contemporary circumstances (John 5:39-40). Eventually, however, as scribes replaced prophets and revelation became a matter of research instead of an inspired experience, "it is written" became the accepted proof of all religious principles, beliefs, and duties.

Jeremiah began to see that God's covenant terms must be written not upon stone tablets, papyrus, or parchment but upon the heart itself, a heart consenting to obey. Each must, inwardly and individually, "know the Lord," and not merely know the book, however sacred. But Judah failed in both respects: the book was misinterpreted, and her heart was unresponsive. Such stubbornness must provoke punishment. Rumors were already reaching Jerusalem of military stirrings in the north, possibly the movements that culminated in the great battle of Carchemish. Jeremiah's vivid description of impending devastation recalls his warning about the Scythians twenty years before (8:10-13; vv. 10-12 repeat 6:12-15).

It was time to seek refuge in the cities, if only to die there (cf. 4:5). Northern frontiers were already overrun; the sounds

of battle could already be heard. And this enemy, like deaf
adders, could never be charmed to tameness (8:14-17).

At this point Jeremiah gives way to heartrending grief.
He appears to think of Judah as sharing the fate of northern
Israel (v. 19). He hears beforehand the bewildered cries of those
who trusted for safety to God's presence in the temple, and
imagines (or recalls) God's firm rejoinder. It is now too late:
the season of opportunity is past. No balm can assuage Judah's
hurt; no physician is sufficiently skilled for what is wrong with
Israel. The passionate patriot feels he can never find tears
enough. He wishes he could escape, if only to a bare overnight
hut on some desert trail, far from the sort of people Judah has
become. He can only weep for the mountains and pastures of
his beloved land, desolate of man, beast, and bird (8:18–9:2,
10; see the NIV).

> *Reflection:* Here we miss in Jeremiah both the anger
> that arms against sympathy and the self-righteousness
> that feels vindicated when others get what they de-
> serve. Inevitably we remember another who wept for
> the city preparing to crucify him.

As the NIV shows (noting the mixed poetry and prose, and
the repeated new headings), the remainder of chapter 9 consists
of separate oracles whose date is quite uncertain, except for the
position assigned to them.

9:11   This is an isolated fragment (note change of tense,
and NIV) in which God pronounces sentence upon Judah.

9:12-16   This passage — suddenly in prose — offers a
blunt question that will be on many lips, and the Lord's equally
forthright answer. The coming exile grows steadily clearer and
more sure.

9:17-21   A separating title sets apart this call for professional "mourning women" to bewail the end of Zion. As
during times of plague, the approach of death cannot be stayed:

it climbs in the very windows, empties the streets, and strikes down the living where they stand. Nothing now can avert the ultimate disaster.

9:22 Again the Lord speaks, adding two more horrifying metaphors to those of 9:11, announcing the same inevitable end.

9:23-24 Contents as well as title separate this profound oracle from its setting. It is one of Jeremiah's greatest sayings. Of all that men boast about in this life, only the knowledge of God is truly precious, and especially the knowledge of his exercise, on earth, of kindness, justice, and righteousness. In these supreme values God himself delights! This is the sum of Jeremiah's religious insight, the foundation of his faith.

But the date and occasion for this gem are wholly speculative. Its form suggests that by the time it was recorded it had become something of a proverb. The saying would form an unanswerable reply to those who, during some temporary lull in danger, mocked the "pessimism" of the prophet and pointed to the wisdom, power, and wealth within the city as its source of security. But that is guesswork. The aphorism stands superbly, timelessly, in its own light.

9:25-26 Here is another treasured saying — the date, occasion, and context of which are unknown — expressing a radical and far-reaching truth. If any in Judah supposed that, for all the prophet's fulminations, God *could not* let his own people, bearing the sacred mark of the covenant, lose their land, go into exile, and end in death, then Jeremiah has a stern answer. Other peoples also bore the same mark — Egyptians, fellow Semites, even Arabs (with their curiously trimmed hair as well!) — without possessing the reality of covenant relationship with God. Thus the rite conferred no security without the covenanted union with God which it was intended to signify. As Paul was to express it, "Circumcision is nothing and uncircumcision is nothing: keeping God's commands is what counts" (1 Cor. 7:19, NIV).

10:1-16 See the Scripture Index.

10:17-22   Only their position, following 9:11-26, links these verses with Jehoiakim's early years, and the intrusion of 10:1-16 makes even that very doubtful. Some think this passage combines detached fragments, since verse 17 anticipates the actual terrors of a siege, whereas verse 22 speaks only of rumor.

The call in verses 17-18 is full of pathos, but final; verses 19-21 suggest a fatalistic acceptance of terminal sickness or injury, a single desert traveler wrestling with a storm, a helpless flock abandoned by incompetent shepherds. Verse 22 dramatically signals the end. In these lines, whenever they were written, it is clear that Jeremiah foresaw destruction and exile as the only cure for Judah's inveterate waywardness.

10:23-25   The cycle of utterances now associated with Jehoiakim's early years closes with yet another of Jeremiah's penetrating comments and prayers. It fittingly summarizes this phase of his ministry in a hostile society. The first and last thing to be said in such a time is that people have proved incapable of ordering their own lives aright. They need divine correction.

Yet, so the prophet prays, if God corrects in anger, humankind will be destroyed. Let God discipline his own people justly, reserving his anger for those who refuse to acknowledge him and those who with excessive violence have destroyed Israel's homeland. (The last words may anticipate the event or reflect hindsight when the utterance was recorded; v. 25 = Psalm 79:6-7.)

Second Period

The fourth year of Jehoiakim was a milestone (see 25:1; 36:1; 45:1; 46:2). At the battle of Carchemish, Nebuchadrezzar broke the sovereignty of Egypt over Palestine and established Babylon as suzerain from the Euphrates to the Nile, including Judah and Jerusalem. Recalled because his father had died and he was to receive the kingship, Nebuchadrezzar at first left the organization of Palestine uncompleted and Jehoiakim a nominal tributary but comparatively independent.

During these four years or so, Jeremiah's ministry was divided between domestic and foreign affairs. He saw the far-reaching consequences of the battle of Carchemish far more clearly than did anyone else in Judah and showed himself "a prophet over the nations" (1:10), especially by his detailed knowledge and breadth of vision (see 25:9, 11).

(i) Foreign Affairs: Jeremiah's "communiques" to surrounding nations, probably sent through their ambassadors in Jerusalem (27:3), were then of urgent relevance, but now are of mainly historical interest. As we have seen, in the Greek Old Testament they occur in a different order and replace 25:14; in Hebrew and English versions they form a "booklet" (46–49/50) under the title of 46:1. Detailed study would need to take notice of numerous variations of text and translation, adjustments made at the time of collection, the odd intermingling of poetry and prose, the use of "Sheshach" (a known code-name for Babylon) in 25:26, the reference to a "book," and the references to Jeremiah in the third person, all of which reveal that these passages have a history of collection and editing as a group. For all that, the general meaning is not obscured.

25:1-38 Despite repeated appeals, Judah has persistently refused to forsake idolatry. God therefore will send for all the tribes of the north and for Nebuchadrezzar — "my servant," God calls him — to punish and destroy Judah along with her neighbors. To the familiar symbols of gaiety and happiness that are to be snatched away, Jeremiah here adds, with pathetic realism, the sound of the millstone by day and the flickering of many candles by night. Without either, any village would be desolate and lifeless indeed (v. 10; cf. 7:34; 16:9; 33:10-11). Total ruin will issue in three generations of slavery (vv. 1-11).

The effect of this widespread devastation is then likened

to a great feast where all the guests are made drunk with the wine of God's wrath; to the sudden attack of a lion upon a defenseless sheepfold, roaring like boisterous grape-treaders; to a great tempest scouring the landscape; and to a vast charnel house. The leaders of the nations especially shall suffer God's wrath because they carry the greater responsibility for past wrongs (vv. 17-37; in v. 34, the RSV's "like choice rams" follows the Greek version; the NIV renders the Hebrew "like fine pottery").

> *Reflection:* Jeremiah here vividly recalls Amos 1–2,
> where also the God of Israel is observer and judge of
> all the nations and sovereign of history — a conviction
> to move the heart and strengthen the hope of modern
> believers, if we can recapture it.

13:12-14   These verses use the same metaphor of "international drunkenness" as the foregoing, though a little differently. They may preserve the origin of the idea. Sitting at a feast and noticing the wine jars, Jeremiah is prompted to utter a trite remark, possibly a proverb or an idle witticism — "Keep them full!" ("Fill 'em up!"). Scornful fellow-revelers ridicule the utterance, but Jeremiah's riposte is sobering: "God will indeed fill them up, and dash them to potsherds, without sparing!" Belshazzar could scarcely have done it better (Dan. 5; in 13:12, the RSV and NEB have "wine jars," but the NIV has "wineskins," in spite of v. 14).

46:1-25/26   Egypt would feel the immediate and heaviest consequences of Carchemish; verses 2-12 exult over Egypt's defeat, pretending to muster Egypt's forces, only to see them flee. Egyptians and mercenaries thought to flood Palestine like the Nile itself at its fullest, but the day was God's, a day of "vengeance" and "sacrifice." As a result, Egypt is fatally wounded.

Now her land itself will be invaded, first her northern cities: Memphis, sacred to Apis the bull, and No (Thebes),

sacred to Amon. Such defeat of Egypt's gods makes the mercenaries desert (v. 16). Pharaoh the boaster "has missed his
opportunity" (v. 17, NIV). Nebuchadrezzar towers like a moun-
tain, or a cliff face; he is a gadfly making the herd frenzied; his
armies are like woodsmen or locusts, destroying all. For Egypt's
warriors are pampered calves that "will turn and flee together,"
like hissing serpents that will slither away through the under-
growth. Shame and capture are certain, for the Lord of armies
will punish not only Egypt's rulers but all who (like the pro-
Egypt party in Judah) have trusted in them (vv. 13-25; a
possible pun on "Hophra" in v. 17 *may* betray that vv. 13-25
were added when the remnant of Judah reached Egypt after
Jerusalem fell; the last words appear to have been added later
still, when it was known that Egypt did not disappear into
Babylon's empire; vv. 27-28 = 30:10-11, here added as a hopeful
postscript; "Jeremiah on Egypt" (vv. 2-26) is evidently a collection in itself).

47:1-7 Philistines occupied the coastal plain over which
Nebuchadrezzar drove southward with overwhelming power,
aiming to weaken Tyre and Sidon by cutting off help from their
ally, Philistia. The reference to Pharaoh in the prose heading is
unexplained; Caphtor = Crete, reputed home of the Philistines.
(Verse five names mourning customs; the Anakim in the RSV
were reputed giants [Num. 13:32-33], but the NIV keeps the
Hebrew "remnant on the plain"; in v. 6 the NIV inserts "you
cry," presumably meaning the Philistines; the RSV and NEB make
Jeremiah answer his own question, that Nebuchadrezzar wields
the sword of God.)

48:1-47 Moab, east of the Dead Sea, will likewise suffer
following Carchemish, though a note of sympathy for Lot's
descendants tempers Jeremiah's warning. But Moab has "mag-
nified himself against the Lord" (v. 42). The list of doomed
cities implies attack from the north, with Heshbon becoming
enemy headquarters, though certain fugitives did not know this

(v. 45). Numerous solemn puns on city names are lost in translation; for instance, the city name "Madmen" sounds like Hebrew "be silenced" (see v. 2).

Verse 6 in the RSV — "Be like a wild ass in the desert," not trusting in strongholds — is clearer than the NIV's "become like a bush in the desert," which may mean surviving despite difficult conditions. In verse 9 in the RSV, "give wings to Moab" may be mockery, but the NIV's "put salt on Moab" is inexplicable. Verse 10 (an inserted prose comment in the RSV, a poetic insertion in the NIV) is probably Jeremiah's sternest utterance. Verse 11 refers to wine soured by standing on accumulated sediment, tasting of the cask; Moab's trust in Chemosh has never been shaken by reverses as Israel's trust in her bull-idol at Bethel was shaken. But Moab's pride and fame are about to be humbled (vv. 14, 17, 29, 42).

Moab's proud character, fertile soil, and famous wines are confirmed elsewhere; for example, the inscription of the Moabite Stone records that sacred vessels from an Israelite temple at Nebo were consecrated to Chemosh by the king of Dibon (see vv. 22, 42). Jeremiah's reproaches seem all the harsher for the regret, weeping, and funeral flutes that lament through the poetry. Yet the eagle (Nebuchadrezzar?) shall certainly end Moab's nationhood (vv. 40-44).

The length of this prophecy; close parallels in Isaiah (chaps. 15, 16); the new "heading" at verse 40; the unexpected note of hope in verse 47, betraying that Moab was not totally destroyed after Carchemish; the absence of verses 45-47 from the Greek version — all suggest that an original prophecy has grown in the hands of Jeremiah's successive collecting disciples (see 2 Kings 24:2; Jer. 40:11; Ezek. 25:8-11). But that the prophecy was preserved at all shows that Moab suffered to some extent.

49:1-6 Ammon, also related to Lot, had varied in attitude from harassing Judah to seeking alliance with her (27:3) and sheltering her refugees (40:11). Earlier, when northern

Israel fell, Ammon annexed her trans-Jordan territory (49:1-2), while a king of Ammon would later plan the assassination of governor Gedaliah, probably hoping to benefit also from Judah's fall.

Against this love-hate background, Jeremiah's message is brief and very like that to Moab. The god Chemosh is replaced by Milcom (so the NEB and the RSV have it, but the NIV has "Molech," with "their king" given as the gloss in the footnote). Rabbah was Ammon's capital; Heshbon was just inside Moab with (apparently) a suburb, Ai, in Ammon. In verse 3, "among the hedges" (RSV), "inside the walls" (NIV) may mean "among sheepfolds" (convenient "fortresses" in open country); the NEB's "score your bodies with gashes" (in mourning?) is unexplained. Total, unhindered evacuation and exile lie ahead; boasted riches will not buy off this enemy. Nevertheless, afterward the Lord will relent — another hopeful "appendix"?

49:7-22 Edom, descendants of Esau and related to Judah, was an age-long enemy, gloating over Israel's every misfortune. Strong, ruthless, shrewd (rather than morally "wise," v. 7), Edom occupied massive highlands south and east of the Dead Sea, with innumerable caves and rocky defiles (vv. 8, 10), and was confident of safety. Yet she too will be mauled like an undefended fold by the Babylonian "lion," torn by the Babylonian eagle, ravaged more thoroughly than by thieves and grape-gatherers. The Lord has already summoned nations to accomplish this (v. 14).

The one faint promise of restoration, though only as "small among the nations" (v. 15), was fulfilled. Edom prospered for several centuries. But she was "despised" among men, her very name a curse. Verse 11 sounds sympathetic, but in the context some think it a sarcastic comment, others a quotation from some Edomite mockery. The one offense here charged against Edom is pride, though old grievances are in the background (v. 16).

So the chapter now runs. But a surprising amount of it

is shared with the book of Obadiah (Obad. 1-6, 8), and the history of that book is too obscure to decide why. Jeremiah 49:17 = 19:8 (of Jerusalem); 49:18-21 = 50:40, 44-46 (of Babylon); 49:22 resembles 48:40-41; 49:12 echoes 25:15-28. Some editorial arrangement is evident, but that the chapter includes Jeremiah's message for the old enemy at this crucial time cannot be doubted.

49:23-27 This somewhat odd poem describes simply the paralysis and fear that seize Damascus at some unexplained bad news, and ends with a prophecy that her youths shall fall and her army be destroyed. A postscript echoes Amos 1:4 in threatening fire upon the palaces of one of her several Ben-hadads, though no charge is laid against Damascus, and she was scarcely a neighbor of Judah, nor was she among the nations addressed in 25:17-26. Verse 25 recalls a later nickname for the city — "Paradise"; translation is especially difficult in verse 23 and verse 25.

Any explanation of the poem's purpose is speculative. *If* Judah supposed that Carchemish was too distant for any battle there to concern her, then an account of the panic in very distant Arpad, almost-as-distant Hamath, and distant, powerful Damascus — as the news of Nebuchadrezzar's triumph filtered southward — might well be Jeremiah's answer.

49:28-33 Kedar was a large Arabian community inhabiting oasis villages; "Hazor" ("village") was the name of several settlements of "the children of the east," the nomads of Arabia. These ancient clans wandered the wilderness between the Euphrates and the Jordan, a danger to Nebuchadrezzar's supply lines in any westward campaign.

Both stanzas of the poem call upon Nebuchadrezzar to attack and plunder the Arab peoples, for in this the new king's plan (v. 30) coincides with God's (vv. 28, 31). So once again Carchemish will affect a neighboring people, though Jeremiah does not charge the Arabs with any crime; the odd tribal mark of trimming the hair over the temples is more a description than an accusation, although the practice was forbidden to Israel (Lev. 19:27).

These varied "international communiques" abundantly confirm Jeremiah's wide knowledge of places and peoples and his insight into the consequences of world events. They illustrate even more the breadth of his theological outlook and the down-to-earth realism that made his vision of God so relevant to the world around him.

(ii) Home Affairs:

13:20-27 Two clues suggest that this passage belongs to the time of Jehoiakim: the expected foe is "from the north" (v. 20), though not now invading marauders but former lovers ("allies," NIV, but note 22:20, 22), now appointed Judah's tyrannical head (v. 21). Jerusalem had long courted Babylon as an ally against Assyria (2 Kings 20:12-18); "lovers" implies the unfaithfulness to God which this heathen friendship involved, and it glances at the lewd practices of hill shrines, again tolerated under foreign influence (vv. 25-27). The following verses dwell on these two forms of Israel's "adultery." So Ezekiel later spelled out Jeremiah's meaning (Ezek. 23:22-27).

After Carchemish, Jeremiah expected these former lovers to arrive as overlords. He addressed Jerusalem, whose "flock" was her citizens or her dependent villages (v. 27, and probably v. 20). The city is a wanton shepherdess whose evil habits have become as much a part of her as dark skin color is to an Ethiopian or spots are to a leopard. She will be humiliated, but Jeremiah almost despairs of any change in her — "almost," because he does hope for her cleansing, though it take a long time.

Reflection: The mills of God grind slowly, but so also, sometimes, move the wheels of grace.

19:1–20:6 The story of the public breaking of an earthenware flask ("jar," NIV) now follows that of the visit to the potter's house, but the connection is literary, not historical. The naming of Babylon as the *imminent* enemy (20:4) and of the high places of Baal place the story in Jehoiakim's reign, after the defeat of Egypt but before Nebuchadrezzar reached the city. (The correspondence of 19:5-7 with 7:31-33 lends some confirmation to this date.)

The "Potsherd Gate" of Jerusalem may have suggested Jeremiah's dramatic action; people and city will be "thrown out" by God like vessels beyond repair (19:11). It is indicative of Jeremiah's sense of responsibility that he chose leaders, lay and priestly, and not the crowd, to witness his declaration of approaching doom. It was their tolerance of defiling idolatry, bloodshed, cult worship, and infant sacrifice which made that doom inevitable.

The desecration of the ancient sacred site with corpses, the horrible poetic justice of verse 9 (cf. Deut. 28:53), and the defiling of the great houses upon whose roofs idolatry had been practiced made the whole city an altar — of *shame* ("Topheth"). All is vividly set forth in the double action of pouring out the contents of the flask, as making empty all Judah's plans for survival, and of breaking the flask into pieces, as indicating Judah's irretrievable brokenness. (So the RSV has it; in v. 7 the NIV substitutes for "make void" the word "ruin," supposing a pun on the Hebrew word for "jar.")

Jeremiah repeated this warning within the court of the temple, with no invitation to repent or hope of reprieve. Nebuchadrezzar was already on his way! As with the earlier temple sermon, the consequences for the prophet were perilous. Pashhur, a priest, temple official, and prophet (20:6), had Jeremiah thrashed and confined to the public stocks overnight. Pain, humiliation, and public ridicule wrung from Jeremiah during the darkest hours of that lonely night one of his sharpest arguments with God (20:7-18) and his sharpest pronouncement upon his enemies. Pashhur ("prosperity on every side") he renamed "terror on every side," recalling his earliest warnings to

Jerusalem and at this point emphasizing how its doom would involve Pashhur, his family, and his party.

> *Reflection:* Nothing is quite so futile and self-defeating
> as meeting truth with violence; often tried, it frustrates
> the persecutors, is costly to the truth-bearers, and al-
> ways convinces more doubters than it deters.

36:1-32 Still in Jehoiakim's fourth year (after Carchemish but before Nebuchadrezzar reached Jerusalem, according to v. 29), Jeremiah was for some reason "restricted" (v. 5, NIV; "debarred," RSV) from attending the temple, though not yet in hiding or in prison (v. 19). No explanation is given, though the foregoing "flask story" may supply it. Jeremiah resolved to make a new appeal to the city authorities. In his youth, a book read within the temple had stirred consciences; could the same strategy, in the renewed danger, kindle memories and move Judah again to turn from evil and be forgiven? (v. 3).

Jeremiah engaged Baruch to record all his former prophecies concerning a foe from the north and the religious and moral decay that left Judah so vulnerable. The task took some months, and then advantage was taken of a national day of fasting and worship, with all Judah at the temple, for Baruch to read the scroll "in the hearing of all the people" (v. 10). That some danger was anticipated is clear from Baruch's use of the room (office?) of a friendly family among the princes.

A member of the same family who was the grandson of the man who first read the law-book to King Josiah reported Baruch's reading to a meeting of princes. They heard the scroll read a second time, asked questions about its authority, and advised that Jeremiah and Baruch go into hiding. The tense atmosphere of the occasion is further revealed by the princes' hiding of the scroll before they brought its contents to the notice of the king.

Jehoiakim in turn desired to hear it read. When Josiah

had heard the law-book read, he had rent his royal robes in dismay and penitence; Jehoiakim contemptuously cut Jeremiah's scroll to pieces as the reading proceeded, burning each piece. He then commanded that Jeremiah and Baruch be arrested, but "the Lord [through the friendly princes] hid them."

The scroll was destroyed, but the prophet was saved; unsilenced, still indomitable, he dictated the whole again, with additions, and included a solemn warning to Jehoiakim. This second scroll (as we have seen) probably underlies earlier chapters of our present book of Jeremiah. The only immediate effect of Jeremiah's appeal was that when Nebuchadrezzar ultimately reached Jerusalem, Jehoiakim recognized the inevitable and surrendered without resistance.

> *Reflection:* Jeremiah's judgment upon Jehoiakim rested especially upon his burning of the scroll, an action that was of a piece with his assassination of Uriah; he *would not* hear the word of God. This is ever the basis of divine judgment: "the light has come . . . [but] men loved darkness" (John 3:19).

Third Period

Jehoiakim's submission lasted just three years. Then he once more attempted to assert some independence, probably by withholding tributary dues, possibly in concert with neighboring allies. Nebuchadrezzar was again preoccupied elsewhere, but he sent bands of Chaldeans, Syrians, Moabites, and Ammonites to teach Jehoiakim a lesson: "The Lord sent . . . bands . . . against Judah to destroy it. . . . Surely this came upon Judah at the command of the Lord" (2 Kings 24:1-4).

12:7-17　This is the situation alluded to in this "islanded"

paragraph. The variation between future and past in the NIV reflects the uncertainty of Hebrew tenses, but the RSV and NEB relate the passage to this harassment by Judah's neighbors at Babylon's instigation. God himself laments what has become of his inheritance; abandoned, antagonistic as a ravening lion, ravaged, trampled, Judah has become a deserted wasteland, for God is angry with her (vv. 7-13).

The agents of destruction are the "evil neighbors" (v. 14), taking advantage of Judah's weakness (and Nebuchadrezzar's absence) to plunder Judah. Thus Judah has become "a speckled bird" (v. 9), mobbed and ostracized by its own flock. The Lord, having lost patience, has "forsaken" and "abandoned" his heritage.

Yet God's agents are not themselves exempt from God's judgments. They too shall be plucked from their homelands and taken into exile. Nevertheless, mercy may prevail. If Judah's neighbors learn her faith and ways as hitherto, unfortunately, Judah had learned theirs, then each may come to be "built up in the midst of" the people of God. But any nation (including Judah) who will not listen will be destroyed (vv. 14-17 — a prose comment upon the poem, with v. 14 explaining v. 9).

> *Reflection:* It is always dangerous to presume upon the
> patience of the living God, whose judgments are as
> sure as they are just, and whose ways are evenhanded
> among all peoples.

35:1-19 Eventually, Nebuchadrezzar himself turned westward, and once more those who could sought refuge in Jerusalem, among them certain "Rechabites" (v. 11). The Rechabites were a family guild who worshipped God strictly after the manner of the pilgrim patriarchs, living as nearly as possible in the nomadic fashion of Abraham, Isaac, and Jacob. Crops, vineyards, houses, towns, and cities all tied men to one place, they said, and so bred luxury, strife of possession, materialism, worship of fertility gods, and all manner of soft, lazy extravagance, very different from the hard, disciplined life of herdsmen under the desert stars. This "back to nature" protest against an enervating "civilization" found expression in Elijah, the Nazarites, and the Feast of Tabernacles (and later in John the Baptist and the Essenes); the Rechabites were especially staunch leaders of the movement, avoiding settled communal living and all indulgence in wine.

With the approach of Babylonian armies, however, these pious "traveling folk" found life so hazardous that they were forced to compromise by seeking refuge within city walls. Their arrival, dress, manner, and abstinences would be a nine days' wonder to city dwellers, and this gave Jeremiah the idea for another vivid object lesson.

Gathering leaders of the Rechabite clan in a room within the temple precinct, he issued a formal invitation to them by name to drink wine with him. With equal formality the Rechabites refused, explaining the commandments laid upon them by their father-founder. Rounding upon the amused spectators, Jeremiah contrasted the faithful obedience of the Rechabites to the rules of their human father and clan with Judah's constant disobedience of the covenant laws of her God. Judah therefore fully deserved all the evils threatened in that covenant; in contrast, the Rechabites would "never lack a man to stand before [the Lord]." This simple story would provide a subject for lively discussion throughout the city for an evening; but for as long as the Rechabites remained in Jerusalem, every individual Rechabite, with his or her curious garb, austere manner, and outlandish accent, would be a walking reminder of the prophet's accusations — which was doubtless what Jeremiah intended.

Reflection: There is always room in society for sincere and humble protest groups who resist the social evils they deplore — extravagance, materialism, sexual promiscuity, pride, drunkenness, militarism — with the example of their own genuine piety and strict abstinence. The cost of such minority witness is often high; its social and spiritual power is immeasurable.

The account of Jehoiakim's last years given in 2 Kings 24 closes with these statements: "So Jehoiakim slept with his fathers, and Jehoiachin his son reigned in his stead. . . . At that time the servants of Nebuchad[r]ezzar came up to Jerusalem . . . And Nebuchad[r]ezzar . . . came to the city, while his servants were besieging it" (vv. 6, 10-11). This implies that Jehoiakim died before the siege began. 2 Chronicles 36:6 (followed by 2 Esdras) says that Nebuchadrezzar bound Jehoiakim in fetters to take him to Babylon — which may be a summary statement of Nebuchadrezzar's intention, which Jehoiakim's death forestalled.

So, to Jeremiah's mind, Babylon's victory at Carchemish heralded the day of judgment for Judah and for all her neighbors. Once again his detailed predictions seemed discredited by delay. For four years Nebuchadrezzar did not come; for another three there was uneasy, partial freedom, with harassment by plundering neighbors. The end was not yet. When Jehoiakim died, he did not, after all, receive "the burial of an ass," but shared the royal sepulcher; and he did have a son to sit upon his throne — if only for three months.

As so often, Jeremiah's story of opposition to a bad king is punctuated by outbursts of perplexed prayer and disappointed faith. Yet, as before, the prophet's basic insight was eventually justified, and his fundamental principles — that the whole earth (not just Judah) was the Lord's, that God's will was to be discerned in the movements of history, that in faithful obedience alone lies security under God's hand — were to be fully vindicated. But not yet.

7

Sympathizing with a Tragic King

Jehoiachin ascended his father's throne at only eighteen years of age, in the midst of siege, and he surrendered to Nebuchadrezzar three months later. He was at once exiled to Babylon, with his wives, his mother, and his servants; princes and palace officials; all military personnel; craftsmen and smiths; and the treasures of temple and palace. The total number exiled is disputed, but it was probably eight thousand (cf. 52:28 with 2 Kings 24:14, 16).

52:31-34 Babylonian records confirm this paragraph, making the year of Jehoiachin's exile 597 B.C., and mention the provision of oil for the king and his five sons on his release (see 1 Chron. 3:17-18).

Jeremiah was not among those transported, perhaps because he was not of the higher social rank or not of military usefulness, or because he was believed to be pro-Babylon in outlook and likely to support the king now being left in charge. This was Jehoiachin's uncle, renamed Zedekiah. Jeremiah offers no criticism of Jehoiachin but shows considerable sympathy for the young king's tragic hundred days' reign.

94

Strangely, Ezekiel speaks of Jehoiachin's martial prowess (Ezek. 19:5-7); 2 Kings 24:9 says that he did "evil in the sight of the Lord, according to all that his father had done." Jeremiah seems to imply that the queen mother exercised undue influence over the young man, setting no better example (13:18). Later generations remembered that Jehoiachin's prompt surrender to Nebuchadrezzar saved the city from destruction for another decade.

The Divine Verdict

13:15-19 In a poem of two stanzas, linked by the common themes of pride and a captivity now regarded as certain, Jeremiah offers an appeal that the approaching darkness and exile be accepted by the king (evidently Jehoiachin) and by the queen mother, with resignation. Let them give God his due place, humbling themselves under his hand. The crown has already fallen from their heads (so the RSV has it in v. 18; the NIV has "will fall"); there is no escape, even southward. If in their pride they refuse to respond, Jeremiah can only weep for the young king, and for Judah.

16:1-21 Only the air of inescapable doom, so like that of the foregoing, offers any hint of the occasion of this prophecy, and that air could well indicate the reign of Zedekiah. But one phrase, "a land which neither you nor your fathers have known" (v. 13), recurs with slight variations at 17:4 and 22:28, verses that also suggest Jehoiachin's brief reign.

It is probable that verse 16 refers to two separate "searchings out" of captives for exile. If this is true, Jeremiah may be warning that the imminent exile of Jehoiachin and his nobles will be only the first; a more thorough transportation, from which none will escape, shall follow. (Verses 14-15 would indicate a later date, when thoughts turned to the hope of return;

but these verses belong at 23:7-8.) Inconclusive as these hints are, no firmer date for 16:1-21 can be suggested.

Jeremiah records that he had been forbidden a wife and family "in view of the present ['impending' in margin] distress" (as Paul expresses it in 1 Cor. 7:26, almost quoting Jeremiah). That distress would fall heavily upon family life, as siege, famine, disease, and warfare always do. The normal, comforting rituals of mourning will be impossible, and any consolation that the prophet might offer is forbidden. It is a dreadful picture of unrelieved misery, with an equally dreadful cause: God has withdrawn his peace, his love, and his mercy (vv. 1-9, RSV; "my blessing, my love and my pity," NIV).

When Judah inquires why God so deals with her, Jeremiah is to recount the sins of the fathers, which the present generation has emulated with increased willfulness. In punishment, God will "hurl" them into an alien land, where (according to popular belief) they must worship alien gods (cf. 1 Sam. 26:19; 2 Kings 5:17). "The lifeless forms of their vile images" (NIV; "the carcasses of their detestable idols," RSV) defile both the mind with idolatry and the land with the uncleanness always associated with death (vv. 10-18).

To this depressing picture of dire punishment fully deserved is added (by Jeremiah, in a change of mood? or by a later collector?) a hopeful ending, hung (as it were) upon that peg of "detestable idols." Remembering the strength and refuge he himself finds in a *living* God, this writer looks to the time when the Gentiles will come confessing that they have inherited only false and worthless gods which are no gods. To this God replies that then they will be taught (at last? or once and for all?) the "power and might" of him whose name is "the Lord" (vv. 19-21; the NIV sets v. 21 as poetry, the RSV as prose).

Reflection: Worshiping "the lifeless forms of vile images" or any other substitute for the living God is religion — of a sort; though it leaves life without hope, comfort, ideals, or gladness. Only the personal knowledge of the living God bestows peace, mercy, love, and everlasting life.

17:1-2; 17:3-4 = 15:13-14   Here again, as in 16:1-21, a sense of finality, of inescapable loss and the prospect of exile, together with the phrase "a land which you do not know" (17:4), suggest that the occasion of these words lies in the weeks of siege and foreboding marking Jehoiachin's short reign. Judah's sin is indelibly recorded, as with an iron carving-tool or a diamond ("flint," NIV) on a stone pillar or copper scroll. But the writing tablet is in literal fact Judah's hardened heart, and the very altars before which Judah worships, and — even worse — the memories of little children.

The chief offense named is idolatry, associated especially with symbols of the mother goddess, practiced still at the countryside hill shrines. The land itself is thereby defiled and the divine covenant broken. The punishment must fit the crime: loss of the inherited treasures of land and status as God's people means return to the slavery from which God had redeemed them. For God's anger is a consuming, and unquenchable, fire.

Reflection: The inscribed record of past sins can be obliterated only by a better inscription: the law of God engraved upon willing hearts under a new covenant.

Accepting the Inevitable

22:20-30   The name "Coniah," a variant of Jehoiachin, in verse 24 and verse 28 places this passage firmly in that king's reign. There is no hope now. God has sworn that even if Jehoiachin were as intrinsically precious and as symbolically important as a signet ring on God's own hand, yet God would snatch it off and throw it into the land of the enemy! The king and his mother together are to be discarded, flung into a far country, never to return (vv. 24-27).

A separate but related poem asks with some sympathy, even indignation, "Is this fair?" Why is the young king treated as a useless potsherd? Jeremiah pleads with the sacred soil itself to listen to the answer: "Such is the Lord's decree." The land and the people have deserved this ultimate disaster. The young king is necessarily involved in the consequences of social wrongs far beyond the measure of his personal responsibility. But those consequences must surely follow from that persistent wrong. It is God's world, and God's law.

> *Reflection:* "No man is an island, entire of itself." For good as well as for ill, individuals are bound in the bundle of life with their community, sharing inevitably in weal and woe, in blessing and judgment.

In his slight and almost hopeless ministry toward Jehoiachin, Jeremiah could do little more than urge acceptance of the situation with humility toward God. There was no time for more. Yet the strange pattern of Jeremiah's experience as a prophet was repeated again. All that he said was the living truth of God, but once more the doom he so vividly described did not fall. Although king, queen, ruling class, and leading people were taken into exile, the city was not destroyed; the state of Judah survived, though no longer with even illusory freedom; a Jewish king still sat on the throne of David. Thus Jeremiah's warnings were yet once more derided as the morbid vaporings of a pathological pessimist.

Yet Jeremiah's greatest ministry lay still ahead.

8

Counseling a Weak King

Zedekiah was only twenty-one years old when, like Jehoia-chin, he inherited an impossible situation. Jerusalem was in Babylon's hands; the ablest counselors were in exile, along with enormous plunder; and, according to Ezekiel 17:13-14, Nebuchadrezzar "made a covenant with him, putting him under oath. (The chief men of the land he had taken away, that the kingdom might be humble and not lift itself up, and that by keeping his covenant it might stand.)"

Zedekiah was less wicked than weak and unwise. Despite the harsh lessons of Megiddo, Carchemish, and the recent exile of Jehoiachin, Zedekiah still had dreams of independence. Jeremiah knew better. His deeply religious mind was far more realistic than those of formalist priests, fanatical prophets, and the foolish king. That realism was the key to Jeremiah's ministry in the dying years of Judah, and to the hostility which it provoked. In addition, his position was gravely weakened by the exile of those intelligent enough to understand him and powerful enough to protect him.

In this period, therefore, Jeremiah was lonelier and more

99

vulnerable than ever, and had fewer illusions. Yet he never ceased to warn that only in surrender could individuals — and only individuals — find security; for the city and the state there was no hope, because Babylon was God's agent in punishing Judah's sinfulness. Nebuchadrezzar himself wrote this idea indelibly upon the minds of king and subjects by naming the king Zedekiah — "the righteousness of God" — thus posing as executor of divine judgment upon a treacherous and forsworn city (40:2-3; cf. Ezek. 17:16-21).

Jeremiah himself believed that the future lay not with the city and the land but with those already exiled. The state, like the temple and its ritual, no longer mattered. The only important consideration was the faith that would survive the Exile and shape the distant centuries. That he should say so, and so forthrightly, inevitably added to the hostility he aroused.

The Story in Outline

The story of Zedekiah's eleven miserable years is soon told. Scarcely had he settled upon the throne when news of Nebuchadrezzar's troubles elsewhere provoked neighboring states to conspire against Babylon's rule. The conspiracy came to nothing, but resisting it placed Jeremiah in new danger.

51:59-64 This passage evidently belongs to this occasion. This puzzling paragraph, bearing the date "the fourth year of the reign of Zedekiah," says (in Hebrew) that Baruch's brother, Seraiah (32:12), went as "quartermaster" ("staff officer," NIV) *with* Zedekiah to Babylon, as though to renew submission; the Greek version says that Seraiah carried tribute *from* Zedekiah. Either form of capitulation might have been demanded to allay Babylon's suspicions. But Jeremiah commissioned Seraiah to carry a scroll containing "all the evil that should come upon Babylon" (v. 60), and, after reading it, to cast it, with prescribed words, into the Euphrates, Babylon's river. The action and ritual suggest the symbolic prophecy that sets in motion what is predicted.

But Jeremiah's purpose is obscure. The action could hardly be made publicly known in Jerusalem, where Jeremiah was urging surrender to Babylon, nor yet in Babylon, where Jeremiah urged the exiles to settle and prosper. Whoever was allowed to know of Seraiah's mission would be convinced that Jeremiah was not, after all, pro-Babylon, though he very often sounded so. This *may* have been Jeremiah's purpose, to reassure his few friends privately that he believed Babylon would yet fall, in God's good time (v. 64: the NIV has "and her people will fall"; the RSV places "and they shall weary themselves" in the margin, as possibly misplaced from v. 58).

Some five years later, when a new pharaoh ruled Egypt, Zedekiah "rebelled against him [Nebuchadrezzar] by sending ambassadors to Egypt, that they might give him horses and a large army" (Ezek. 17:15). This time Nebuchadrezzar arrived promptly. Believing that the city was invulnerable (21:13) and that the temple ensured safety, Judah offered resistance for a year and a half. At one point, an Egyptian force threatened to approach, and the main Babylonian army withdrew to meet it, events once more apparently contradicting Jeremiah's warnings. But the Babylonians soon returned.

Throughout the siege, Jeremiah was treated as an enemy within the gates, a traitor friendly to Babylon, his life and liberty constantly threatened. Zedekiah himself was afraid to harm Jeremiah and consulted him secretly, though he was too weak and indecisive to obey him. Sympathy once again tempered the prophet's judgment. When at last a breach was made in the walls, the king attempted to escape, but he was captured, blinded, and taken in chains to Babylon. The city was destroyed. The catastrophe that Jeremiah had prophesied

for forty years had now fallen, but vindication did not prove
sweet — Jeremiah's own heart was broken.

The First Six Years

23:1-8; 16:14-15 The former verses (which include the latter)
are now attached to other oracles about Judah's kings. The only
indication of date is the play upon the name "Zedekiah."
Jeremiah is commenting on this intriguing name ("the righteousness of God"), reversing its syllables to coin a title for the
ideal king who shall one day replace these weak or wicked kings
who have brought the people of God to such desperate straits.
This king, at least, will deserve this wonderful title.

This interpretation carries much greater conviction if we
recall Jeremiah's fondness for such Hebrew "puns." The
"Branch" or "Shoot" (from David's "stock") was a familiar title
for the Messiah (Isa. 11:1; later Zech. 3:8; 6:12); attributes of
wisdom and righteousness, and the task of "shepherding" God's
people, were also part of the Messiah's image. It is significant
that here Jeremiah blames not Zedekiah but the rulers (princes,
"shepherds") against whom the king was so helpless.

Such a comment on the king's name might be appropriate
at the time of his flight and exile, though circumstances and
mood might then make it tasteless. More probably, the comment
was made when the new name was first announced. The unexpected promise of a return (23:3, 7-8) and a future life in their
own land under a king *deservedly* called "Zedekiah" seem to be
implied in the promise of "caring shepherds" (v. 4). These would
have no function without flocks to tend, as the Messiah also
would need a people to rule. Thus the whole prophecy looks far
ahead — a prophetic glimpse of further meanings in present
events, just such as came to Jeremiah with the almond blossom
and the boiling pot, the potter's vessel and the refilled wine-jars.

The glimpse seems hardly to belong among Jeremiah's thundering warnings of total ruin. So perhaps this, too, was privately expressed (see 51:59-64).

> *Reflection:* The great "Messianic hope" sprang primarily from repeated disappointment with earthly kings; disillusionment need not always engender despair: it sometimes serves to refine hope and clarify our expectations.

49:34-39 Elam was an ancient kingdom that in its time had fought both Assyria and Babylon. Given its position at the head of the Persian Gulf, it might seem too remote to engage Jeremiah's interest. Nor does the presence of Elamites among the mixed population of Samaria, and probably in the armies of Nebuchadrezzar, sufficiently explain this oracle. But from the fairly common adoption of the name "Elamites" by Jews after the Exile and the presence of Jews in Elam long afterward (Acts 2:9), it is probable that some of the exiles who accompanied Jehoiachin found themselves in this distant corner of the Babylonian empire.

That would explain Jeremiah's prophesying "in the beginning of the reign of Zedekiah" concerning Elam's future, using words now preserved among other "oracles concerning the nations." The message is almost entirely threatening: Elamites were famous archers, but their bow will be broken, the people scattered, and Elam will know the anger of the Lord. Indeed, God will set his throne of judgment within her borders to destroy her king and princes.

Yet eventually Elam will be restored (another intrusive hopeful ending?). Meanwhile, the oracle offered a crumb of comfort to those people of Judah already in exile, indicating that God's judgment would reach even to Elam when his favor turned again toward his people. So far from home, but not from God! (cf. Isa. 5:25; 9:12, 17, 21).

Reflection: For justice, as for mercy, "the arm of the Lord is not too short" (Isa. 59:1, NIV); life may carry us far away, but far away from where — from what?

24:1-10 The opening verses of this clear utterance place it soon after the deportation of Jehoiachin and his fellow exiles. The reference to Jews in Egypt (v. 8) does not contradict this. Extra-biblical sources witness that from the sixth century onward Jews dwelt in Egypt, among them possibly those who accompanied Jehoahaz and any of the pro-Egypt party in Judah who fled for refuge at the approach of Nebuchadrezzar.

The "vision" (v. 1, RSV) was probably another ordinary incident (in the fruit market?) that "spoke" to the receptive mind of the prophet. The oracle is of far-reaching importance: it declares that the favor of God, the whole promise of the future, the assurances of a changed heart in the people of God and of the ultimate fulfillment of the ancient covenant (v. 7) — all are centered firmly upon the *exiled* portion of Judah, while all imaginable evil, including final destruction, will fall on those who have remained in Jerusalem (cf. Ezek. 11:16-21, and see the commentary on Jer. 29:16-20, pp. 107-8).

Such words would be deeply resented in Jerusalem. The sharpness of verses 8-10 expresses the self-righteous assumption of those who had not been carried into exile that they were less sinful and more necessary to God's purposes than those who had been taken away. Jeremiah seems to imply that he, and God, shared Nebuchadrezzar's view that the remnant in Jerusalem were of no importance.

Of course, those already in Babylon included most of Jeremiah's supporters. But his view was important, partly for its assurance that Judah had a future, a place in the long-range purposes of God, and partly for the implication that the experience of exile would purify this part of God's people once and for all (v. 7). Henceforth *their* religious life would concentrate wholly upon their covenant-keeping God. So the Exile would, after all, prove to be not punishment only but a refining and a new beginning.

Such was the wonderful word of encouragement sent to the desponding exiles, homeless, separated, "discarded," rejected, feeling themselves no longer part of the people of God: "The future depends on you! Hold fast; await God's time. The future is *yours.*"

> *Reflection:* "*All* things work together for good to them that love God" (Rom. 8:28, KJV) — even defeat, exile, and punishment. For God's purposes are always positive: that is the nature of love.

27:1–28:17 Jeremiah's thought of the exiles as "the good figs" shaped his whole conception of the future and the resulting policy of collaboration with Babylon. This policy directly contradicted the counsel of most of the professed prophets and the hopes of civil leaders still dreaming of independence. Thus, when in Zedekiah's fourth year (28:1) envoys arrived from five neighboring states seeking an alliance against Babylon, Jeremiah expressed his opposition to such madness in inspired form (27:1-7).

By going about the city wearing a wooden yoke bound upon his shoulders, Jeremiah declared that the yoke of Babylon lay upon the Middle East by the will of God, and would remain there until God removed it. To resist this divine decree only invited divine punishment, Jeremiah insisted, whatever "your prophets, your diviners, your dreamers, your soothsayers, or your sorcerers" might say (to include prophets in such company was insulting!). Safety for *all* the neighboring states lay in surrender and cooperation. Jeremiah repeated this pronouncement to Zedekiah himself, adding that prophets who counseled otherwise were lying (27:8-15).

The warning was repeated also to priests and the people, especially to contradict the promise of the "prophets" that the temple treasures would shortly be returned. "Let the prophets who so predict pray rather that the rest of the treasures shall not be plundered," Jeremiah said in effect. For God had said that these also would be taken and would remain in Babylon until God would choose to return them (27:16-22).

Later that year, Hananiah, evidently well known as "the prophet from Gibeon," arrived in the city to confront Jeremiah, who still wore his yoke. Hananiah promised the return of king, people, and treasures within two years, for God would break the yoke of Babylon. Gibeon was a priests' inheritance, and thus two priest-prophets stood publicly opposed in a time of religious and political tension (28:1-4).

Jeremiah courteously assented to the general *desire:* "Amen! May the Lord do so!" But he added that according to all precedents, the true prophet had been known for bringing unwelcome, not welcome, words; he who says what is popular will be known for true only if his word is fulfilled. In answer, Hananiah broke Jeremiah's yoke, to symbolize and set in motion the breaking of Babylon's rule. *And Jeremiah walked away* (28:5-11).

Was Jeremiah confused? Did he wait upon time and the event to reveal who was right? Or did he agree that the suggested two years' delay would at least avoid any mad, impulsive adventure of independence? The clear difference between rival religious authorities was evident to all, but was not at that moment acrimonious.

But if Jeremiah had experienced any temporary doubt, his conviction soon cleared. He returned to declare that God would strengthen further the yoke of Babylon over all the would-be conspirators. And he warned Hananiah that because he spoke without God's commission and persuaded Judah to trust in lies, he would die within the year. The prompt fulfillment of this prophecy vindicated Jeremiah and put an end to the movement toward rebellion (28:12-18; see further the commentary on 23:9-40, pp. 108-11).

> *Reflection:* Not all divine truth is doom-laden! But Jeremiah was right: "Time tests truth," whereas the search for popularity betrays it.

29:1-32 Those already in exile also had their prophets promising swift return. Revolutionary excitement was as dangerous there as in Jerusalem, especially if some impulsive action were taken before news of the conspiracy's failure could reach them. Possibly at the prompting of Jeremiah, Zedekiah was sending a deputation to Nebuchadrezzar to explain away rumors of sedition. Jeremiah took the opportunity to send to the restless exiles the warning that he had published in Jerusalem — that the Exile would be prolonged (vv. 1-9).

Accordingly, Jeremiah advised them to settle, prosper, and multiply with at least three generations in view, taking advantage of the freedom, social status, and opportunities for work and progress granted to them as "resident aliens." He repudiated the "lying dreams" that they encouraged their prophets to preach to them. His sharp exhortation is reinforced, however, with very gracious promises for the somewhat distant future. Jeremiah is obviously still thinking of the exiles as bearers of the future and of the Exile as a refining process requiring time (vv. 10-14).

In reply to any claim that the exiles had their own prophets and needed no counsel from Jeremiah (v. 15), he appears to offer an irrelevant paragraph (vv. 16-19). This the Greek version omits; modern translations include it, but with broken sentences and adjusted pronouns; and others regard it as belonging to 24:8-10, because of the reference to bad figs. There is a possible explanation. Probably the prophets of the exiles promised them a return to their Davidic king, a safe city, and a resumed place among God's people, and to counter this alluring prospect Jeremiah summarized what he had been saying in Jerusalem: that the king and the people left in Jerusalem were doomed to further sword, famine, and pestilence, were like bad figs fit only to be thrown away. There was *no hope at all* of rejoining the present state of Judah: it would soon be destroyed.

Jeremiah adds stern forecasts of what will happen to three of the exiles' prophets. Two will be delivered up to Nebuchadrezzar, presumably for encouraging sedition; Jeremiah accuses them also of folly, fornication, and fraud, warning that "God knows all" (vv. 15-23).

The third prophet (v. 31) had written in his own name (v. 25) to the temple authorities at Jerusalem, rebuking them for not silencing Jeremiah and labeling the message received from him as the words of a "madman." The recipient, however, showed this letter to Jeremiah, who replied with further vigorous rebuke and warning (vv. 24-32; the Greek version and the RSV's "not have any one . . . to see" the good that God is planning for the present exiles is preferable to the NIV's "nor will he see," since Shemaiah could hardly live another seventy years).

That Jeremiah was shown Shemaiah's letter suggests that he had gained some respect — or at least inspired superstitious awe — in Jerusalem since his prophecy of the death of Hananiah had been so promptly fulfilled. But this is scarcely an acceptance that Jeremiah would desire, and in other circles it would certainly increase the hatred that endangered his life.

> *Reflection:* The underlying problem of this rivalry remained: in such a time, amid discordant religious voices, how are ordinary people to distinguish true prophets from false? More must be said, but in the last resort it takes spiritual insight to recognize divine inspiration.

23:9-40 Jeremiah had more to say about disagreeing prophets (see the two foregoing passages). In seeking to discern

which prophet speaks God's truth, the nature of the message
— realistic and forthright or popular and people-pleasing — is
certainly relevant (28:7-8); so is vindication by events (28:9)
and the character of the messenger (29:23). Integrity is essential
to inspiration: since God is holy and good, holiness and goodness must be reflected in those who reveal him. This fuller
discussion of the question might have been uttered at various
times; in our book of Jeremiah it has been arranged to follow
"good and bad politicians"! But such discussion had special
relevance for the conflict of counsel during Zedekiah's reign,
when the king's infirmity of purpose made clear counsel so
much more important.

Jeremiah's own authority was not above challenge. He
appeared to contradict the great Isaiah about the security of
Jerusalem; he supported and then criticized the reforms of
Josiah; his predictions of the coming of the Scythians, then
of Nebuchadrezzar after Carchemish, and again of the imminent fall of Jerusalem had all failed. His general policy of
surrender seemed wholly disloyal. During Zedekiah's early
years the contention over who truly spoke for God was far
from academic.

Moreover, Jeremiah himself found prophesying an overwhelming strain (v. 9), and sometimes doubted. The leaders of
religion had brought a curse upon the land and defilement upon
the temple by practicing "adulteries" — in view of the
Canaanite cults, probably literal and figurative adulteries. They
have misled Judah even more treacherously than Samaria's false
prophets, misguiding them to paths slippery and dark. Like
Sodom and Gomorrah, they have poisoned the land with un-
godliness, and they will be given poison in return (vv. 9-15).

Such men should not be given a hearing. They feed people
with vain hopes based only upon "visions" ("their own inven-
tions," v. 26, NEB). Mere time-servers, they avoid rebuking evil,
thus encouraging the rebellious. Not one of them has stood

within "the council of the Lord" (v. 18) to learn his mind; ever eager to comfort, they never understand God's anger — but they will! They talk much but never listen. Had God sent them, they would turn people from evil instead of condoning it (vv. 16-22).

But God is not our equal and familiar: he fills heaven and earth, and knows the secrets of all hearts. He is not to be mocked, duped, or escaped. And to be his spokesman is not a task to be lightly undertaken merely by mouthing the cant-slogans that assert authority: "I've had a dream," "says the Lord," "the Lord has laid a burden upon me." Such claims, once genuine, were by Jeremiah's time discredited, cheapened by flippant reiteration. His charge against such "dreamers" is that they fashion God after their own hearts, making people forget God's true "name" — what he is really like. The given, objective word that "comes" to a man must be sharply distinguished from a man's own imaginings; that true word may be recognized in what nourishes, kindles, and breaks down, as situation and need may require (vv. 25-29).

Some so-called prophets merely retail the secondhand ideas they get from others, yet glibly declare "thus says the Lord"; others chatter endlessly about "the burden of the Lord," though they show no sign of grieving over Judah or of struggling with unwelcome truth. Such prophets are themselves "burdensome," even to God! Why cannot people speak plainly when they ask for God's word and when they utter "the words of the living God"? (Verses 30-40, RSV, NEB; the NIV substitutes "oracle" for "burden," the Hebrew word bearing both meanings. But "oracle" confuses the passage — see vv. 33, 39 — and makes Jeremiah condemn his own practice [see chaps. 3, 5]; the punning ambiguity is probably deliberate.)

The whole argument constitutes a heavy indictment of self-appointed, self-serving "prophets" who usurp and betray a vocation that a confused and imperiled age desperately needs to reverence. Throughout this passage we sense the inner indignation of one who never wished to be a prophet, never wanted to utter the stern message given to him, and who found every new commission a disappointment. But we feel too the sense of true vocation, which made him defend so stoutly a divine calling that he neither enjoyed, boasted of, nor felt free to disobey.

Reflection: "If you utter what is precious, and not what is worthless, you shall be as my mouth" (15:19).

The End Approaches

21:1-10 Among those whose respect, or fear, for Jeremiah had increased must be reckoned King Zedekiah. With Nebuchadrezzar approaching once more, Zedekiah turned pathetically to Jeremiah asking counsel, but evidently hoping that the prophet would achieve a divine deliverance like that which Isaiah obtained for Hezekiah when Sennacherib threatened (vv. 1-2; cf. Isa. 37:36-37). The occasion was that foolish appeal by Zedekiah to Egypt for horses and an army (Ezek. 17:11-21), and Jeremiah may well have thought that Zedekiah deserved to be attacked.

Certainly, Jeremiah's reply was uncompromising, designed to frighten king and people into surrender, so avoiding bloodshed. Any forays outside the city would be defeated; the enemy would eventually enter. Meanwhile, famine and plague would intensify the city's misery and ensure Babylon's victory (vv. 3-7; for conditions within the city toward the end, see 52:4-6). The harsh choice is laid before the people (not the king only) in terms that recall the "book of the law" (Deut. 30:15, 19). For Jerusalem has a fiercer enemy than even Nebuchadrezzar: God himself has become her foe (vv. 5, 8-10).

Reflection: For centuries, Israel's liturgy had repeated this warning: "Today, if you hear his voice, do not harden your hearts." But "today" does not last forever.

37:1-10 It seemed that Zedekiah's hopes (see the foregoing) were to be fulfilled. Egypt's forces approached, and the siege of Jerusalem was slackened as Nebuchadrezzar moved to repulse them. The historical summary describing this situation (vv. 1-5) reads like a new start; it probably once introduced another small collection of Jeremiah memoirs now incorporated in the book of Jeremiah.

This illuminating passage records Jeremiah's new freedom to move about at this time, the movements of Egyptian and Babylonian forces, and the prophet's warning that the respite was only temporary. That warning is stark, almost insulting, and Zedekiah's request for prayer is not even answered. Still more important, the passage illumines the background of three further incidents of great significance in Jeremiah's story:

(i) One of these incidents involves the purchase of a field, which must concern us later.

(ii) **34:1-22** Early in Nebuchadrezzar's attack, when only Jerusalem and two other cities were holding out, Jeremiah sent yet another warning of defeat to Zedekiah, but this time added a personal promise that he would be granted a peaceful death with appropriate royal rites. This seems to have been evoked by Zedekiah's attempting, in his distress, to obey the requirement of the law-book that Hebrew slaves be liberated at the close of six years' service. The law had fallen into abeyance, if it had ever been obeyed, and Zedekiah resolved to go beyond its demand as a public gesture of returning to the covenant (vv. 1-10).

Human motives are usually mixed. Piety and penitence apart, the king's action had prudential advantages. Freed slaves need not be fed, and they could join laborers and soldiers in defending the city. But the general emancipation was given religious formality: a covenant was drawn up, dedicated in the temple, and registered (vv. 8-10). The ancient ritual of covenant-making, walking together between the pieces of a dismembered "sacrifice," was solemnly enacted (vv. 18-19; cf. Gen. 15:10).

Unfortunately for the slaves, the siege was lifted at the approach of the Egyptians (v. 22), and the emancipation was revoked, the new covenant was forgotten, and the slaves were reclaimed (vv. 11, 16). This was "profanation," a broken oath, the violating of a covenant made before God, persistent disobedience, and also social cruelty. Then the word came upon Jeremiah that the city no longer had any hope.

Zedekiah would be spared immediate execution, but the rest would suffer severely: the freedom they had promised the slaves would be turned upon them — "behold, I proclaim to you liberty to the sword, to pestilence, and to famine" (v. 17); they would be dismembered and left to the jackals and vultures, like the calf they had desecrated; just as they had ordered their slaves to return to servitude, so God would order the Babylonians to return to the siege. Judah would pay dearly for her latest breach of covenant (vv. 17-20, 11, 22 literally).

Reflection: "When the devil was ill, the devil a monk would be": religion based upon fear or tragedy, kindled by immediate circumstances, rarely outlives the panic.

(iii) **37:11-21** Taking advantage of the lull in the siege (see the foregoing), Jeremiah attempted to leave the city to go to his home district of Benjamin, but he was immediately arrested by Irijah, a sentry (RSV; "captain of the guard," NIV), and charged with deserting to the enemy. That risk was so obvious that Jeremiah must have felt a pressing need for such a venture (note 38:19). An obscure Hebrew phrase in verse 12

(RSV: "to receive his portion there"; NIV: "to get his share of
the property . . . there"; NEB: "to take possession of his patri-
mony") almost certainly means that he was short of money and
needed his priestly dues, which were accumulating at Anathoth
(vv. 11-13; cf. Num. 18:8).

Another beating, a charge before the authorities (no longer
including friendly princes as that group had some fifteen years
before), and a lengthy imprisonment followed. Eventually,
Zedekiah had Jeremiah brought to the palace for a secret consultation, since the aging prophet was the only remaining source
of hope or counsel. But the king received only the old, consistent warning. Jeremiah also took the opportunity to challenge his unjust imprisonment, to recall how utterly false the
king's preferred counselors had proved to be, and to plead release
from his prison lest he die (vv. 14-20).

Zedekiah evidently accepted Jeremiah's sincerity and
authority, yet he was afraid to follow his advice. He arranged
a form of house arrest for Jeremiah, holding him within the
precincts of the palace (32:2) under military guard, and giving
him a small allowance of bread so long as the city had any
(v. 21).

> *Reflection:* It sometimes takes as much sincerity and
> courage to *hear* the word of God as to *speak* it.

38:1-28; 39:15-18 The city authorities who had committed Jeremiah to prison (see the foregoing) would not consent
to see him slip through their fingers by the intervention of the
king. Moreover, Jeremiah, while under house arrest, still voiced
with undaunted courage his counsel of surrender. It was easy
to represent this as militarily dangerous, undermining morale,
and the leaders demanded Jeremiah's death (38:1-4).

Zedekiah sought to evade responsibility by confessing his
helplessness, but the princes also were afraid to lay murderous

hands upon a prophet. So they lowered Jeremiah into a cistern deep with mud, from which Ebed-melech, with the king's connivance, rescued Jeremiah (see "Jeremiah's Friends" in Chapter 4 of this volume, pp. 38-39). Once again Zedekiah secretly consulted Jeremiah, swearing to protect him, but even now the prophet could offer only the old advice: "Surrender spells safety; resistance means ruin" (38:5-18). Zedekiah confessed his fear that surrender would leave him victim to Babylon's vengeance and to that of the Jews who had already deserted. Jeremiah promised that his life would be spared if he surrendered, but if he would not surrender, then a dreadful fate awaited him, his wives, and his sons, as well as the city. It was an appalling choice to make (38:19-23).

Jeremiah and the king, now strange, unequal conspirators, arranged to keep their consultation secret, even though the princes promised Jeremiah his life if he would disclose it. Jeremiah returned to military custody, and "remained in the court of the guard until the day that Jerusalem was taken" (38:24-28).

> *Reflection:* Wickedness, folly, weakness — all frustrate God's purpose and bring people to ruin. But which does so most often?

Here Jeremiah's *public* ministry ended. But as for so many of God's servants, the darkness of a cell brought its own illumination, and confinement of the body brought liberation of the soul. Alone with God and a menacing future, Jeremiah did some of his deepest thinking *and found his message for all time.*

9

"A Future and a Hope"

When Jeremiah was confined to the guards' court for the last year or so of Jerusalem's agony, he could scarcely have been less than sixty years of age, much worn by privation, beatings, disappointment, strife, a demanding vocation, and little reward. Yet from that enfeebled body and dejected spirit was to come Jeremiah's greatest contribution to the world's religious thought. For his prison-house became his Patmos.

Prison does not of itself generate far vision and profound optimism. Promising strands of thought must be present already before solitude and confinement can weave them into shining hope. It was difficult for Jeremiah to combine relentless warning of disaster with hints of promise, but such gleams were scattered among his darker utterances, waiting to be recalled and re-examined amid the lonely darkness and foreboding of those last months in Jerusalem.

Foregleams

Too much must not be made of phrases like "yet I will not make a full end" (4:27) and the oft-repeated "I will restore the fortunes of . . ." — of Moab, Ammon, Edom. These often contradict preceding warnings and may reflect the hindsight of those who preserved the prophecies; they may even represent the hopeful comments with which rabbis closed the public reading of grim passages in the synagogues.

More definite gleams of hope in Jeremiah's earlier ministry include his insistence upon the divine covenant that Judah had broken. Judah had no claim upon God, but the divine promise was precisely that — a *divine* promise. Reference to the return of the temple vessels (27:22); to the ultimate punishment of Babylon (25:12); to the good which God would do for his people, which Shemaiah would not see (29:32); to the coming of one who shall *deserve* to be called "the righteousness of God" (23:5-6) — all imply that the fall of Jerusalem will not mark the end of Judah.

So does Jeremiah's belief that the exiles already in Babylon are the "good figs" on whom the future rests; they are to be brought back, "built up," planted again, and changed (24:6, 7). The letter to these exiles suggesting that a term of seventy years will elapse before their return has the same implication (29:10; cf. 27:7). Jeremiah could even speak of other nations one day learning the value of knowing a *living* God (16:19-21). Despite all his forthright warnings, Jeremiah still clung to God's title as "the hope of Israel" (14:8; 17:13; see also 50:7), and he could pen this beautiful promise: "I know the plans I have for you, says the Lord, plans for welfare and not for evil, *to give you a future and a hope*" (29:11, emphasis mine).

Nevertheless, all these foregleams of the future do not add up to an eschatology, especially against the background of Jeremiah's persistent talk of ruin, devastation, "sword, famine, pestilence," an empty land, a destroyed city, exile, and divine rejection. Doubtless Jeremiah sometimes hoped against hope; at other times he strongly argued God's case for "avenging himself on a nation such as this" (5:1-31; 9:3-9). It was a very odd event, self-contradictory and inexplicable, which stabbed Jeremiah's spirit broad awake to ponder what the future held. His cousin, Hanamel, arrived, almost certainly as a refugee seeking shelter within the city while Babylon's temporary withdrawal offered the opportunity to do so. And he brought a strange proposition.

A Field for Sale

32:1-44; 33:1-9   The thirty-four years since Jeremiah was last at Anathoth had seen changes, one of which, by Jewish rules of inheritance, left Jeremiah holding the option to purchase a field that might otherwise be sold outside the family. Jeremiah's cousin proposed that Jeremiah should buy it.

But what has an aged prophet, in prison in a beleaguered city, awaiting that city's destruction, to do with buying property? And property lying beyond the city, in an area occupied by the enemy, at that! Stranger still, Jeremiah was "told by God" that Hanamel was coming and his reason for coming, so that when Hanamel proposed the purchase of the property, Jeremiah "knew that this was the word of the Lord" (32:6-8).

So Jeremiah did as he was bidden, with all due formalities of purchase and conveyance, in the presence of named witnesses, and carefully arranged for the preservation of the record. (Clay tablets have been found inscribed as indicated in this passage, and enclosed within clay "envelopes" that also bear the terms of purchase "openly" for easy reference.)   And in the hearing of all concerned, Jeremiah drew an immediate inference, apparently with wonder: "For thus says the Lord of hosts, the God of Israel: Houses and fields and vineyards shall again be bought in this land" (32:9-15).

The action itself, according to current thought, was another symbolic declaration of a truth initiating its own fulfillment. But all the circumstances are perplexing. As the introduction to the story rehearses (strongly suggesting that at some point it circulated on its own), Jeremiah had repeatedly insisted that God was about to give all of Judah into the hand of the king of Babylon (32:1-5). The land is therefore worthless, and the record so elaborately arranged would be pointless: even if Jewish ownership were acknowledged under Babylonian law, it could not be proved — all witnesses would be either dead or exiled! (A similar story, of a Roman soldier who during Rome's wars with Carthage bought "at its full market value" the ground upon which Hannibal's troops were stationed, was retailed for many years as something quite extraordinary.) So, too, Jeremiah believed himself to be *commanded by God* to invest in the very problematic future.

In the most detailed — even verbose — fashion we are told that the contradiction greatly bewildered Jeremiah. Despite his comment before the witnesses, when alone the prophet turns to God with urgent questioning. He rehearses the power and fairness of God; surely, then, his problem is not too hard for such a God! He recalls Israel's unfaithfulness, God's judgments upon her, and comes at last to his bewilderment: "*Yet* thou, O Lord God, hast said to me, 'Buy the field . . .' — though the city is given into the hands of the Chaldeans" (emphasis mine). This "internal" discussion proves that hitherto the future had not been clear to Jeremiah (32:16-25).

The Lord's reply, almost audibly given in the process of Jeremiah's mental debate, is equally full and elaborate. *The moment was obviously crucial,* its implications far-reaching, and the new perspective hard to accept. As usual with Jeremiah, it was essentially the struggle of an honest mind between realism and faith that brought enlightenment. Jeremiah's former assertions are fully confirmed: the fate of the city and God's reasons for anger are rehearsed yet again; Jeremiah has not been wrong. But — *"Behold"* — the buying of the field means something new (32:26-37; note "now" in v. 36).

The new vision is of God's *ultimate* purposes for this land and people, for both Israel and Judah (32:30). Those purposes are wholly gracious and eloquently expounded. God's people will be regathered and will dwell safely again in Israel under a re-established covenant, for "they shall be my people, and I will be their God" (32:38). They shall be given "one heart and one way," they and their children, to fear God forever. And he will rejoice in doing them good with all his heart and soul (32:36-41).

This is the new revelation, the opening of the heavens and of the future, granted to the frail old prophet in his prison. This is the meaning of, and the reason for, the buying of the field held by the enemy: when the punishment is past, the cloud lifted, the lesson learned, again fields shall be bought, agreements shall be kept, ownership shall be acknowledged, and life shall resume its normal course. "I will restore . . . ," says the Lord; the future shall be bright (32:42-44).

In the following chapter we read that God spoke to Jeremiah again: "The word of the Lord came to Jeremiah a second time, while he was still shut up in the court of the guard" (33:1). This time the thought begins with God as maker, and therefore Lord, of all the earth. God offers to reveal to Jeremiah new and hidden things. For example, the damage now being done to property in the besieged city, in order to strengthen its defenses with "borrowed" materials, will yet be repaired. The Babylonians will certainly take the city. But the same stones and timber will still be available for rebuilding when God restores Judah's fortunes, cleanses her guilt, renews the state, and makes Jerusalem once more a joy, startling the neighboring nations by the wonderful reversal of Judah's experience (33:2-9).

This seems a somewhat pedestrian, tradesman-like (or Nehemiah-like) consideration to occupy the prophet at this time: the possible re-use of old materials to rebuild the ruins. It is not impossible that Jeremiah thought also, figuratively, of the rebuilding of the people of God from the same battered, tried, and punished elements as of old. But the literal meaning is striking enough. From the court of the guard where he was being held, the prophet could watch dwellings being demolished to strengthen the city walls, and we know how watching simple, everyday things — almond trees, pots, wine-jars — could stir moments of insight and make truth "dawn" upon his receptive mind. And here the dawning truth confirmed the incident of the field. The prophet's thoughts are fixed now on the distant future — beyond the siege and the fate of the city, beyond the years of exile — upon what God intends for Judah when all the present has passed into history. What then shall be, when, at last the stubbornness of Judah shall have been overridden by the age-long, unswerving purposes of God?

> *Reflection:* Jeremiah's bewilderment is not unique. God loves to surprise his servants with mercies greater than they ask or think. "No eye has seen, no ear has heard, no mind has conceived what God has prepared for those who love him" (1 Cor. 2:9, NIV).

An Anthology of Hope

30:1-3 The result of Jeremiah's bewilderment and illumination (see the foregoing) was another book (chaps. 30-33), which has been called "Jeremiah's little book of comfort," though it deserves a far more respectful title. One hundred and thirty-four verses of moving poetry, solid argument, and eloquent descriptions of the coming restoration of *both* Israel and Judah leave no doubt that Jeremiah "dip't into the future, far as human eye could see" and discerned the ultimate mercies of God.

Doubts about the date of some of these pieces are best considered as each passage is examined. Two portions are repeated from earlier years; a few presuppose that the city has already fallen; some may reflect Jeremiah's sad years in Egypt. The faint foregleams of hope in earlier parts of the book of Jeremiah effectively remove any assumption that Jeremiah could never have been so optimistic, while the story of the purchase of the field convincingly explains his new, exulting hope. The separate passages are distinguishable by their headings — "This is what the Lord says" (used fifteen times), "The word of the Lord came . . ." (used six times), "Behold, the days are coming when . . ." (used four times), and some others — and also by the sudden changes of theme or style.

Clearly, the little book grew by stages, an anthology of hope gathering together memories of the master's teaching on the future. If the result occasionally reveals here and there the collector's hindsight, we need not assume that the prophet's mind has been seriously misrepresented. The command to record what God was now to give provides both the anthology's title and its main themes (vv. 1-4). This introduction was evidently provided after the Exile had begun.

The Future of Israel

30:4-11 Present fears, like the anguish of birth or a day of great distress, shall have an end. Verses 8-9 (poetry in the NIV, a prose intrusion in the RSV and NEB) picture captives yoked together and marching into servitude, but that too shall end;

verses 10-11 reflect the feeling of people in a distant, alien land, but the Lord is with them even there. All is happening "in just measure," which again implies an end and a restoration after due punishment. (Verses 10-11 may have been a well-remembered assurance: see 46:27-28; 10:24.)

The descriptions and assurances are appropriate to the day of Jerusalem's distress, as the position of the poem also suggests. Yet, apart from the heading, the address is to "Jacob," "Israel" (vv. 7, 10). Taken alone, that would imply the northern kingdom and the earlier exile, which still continued. It is true that "Jacob" came to be used of all the exiled Jews, as in later Isaiah, and Jeremiah may be using the term in that sense here. Or the poem may originally have belonged to the first years of Jeremiah's ministry, when the fate of northern Israel was certainly fresh in the prophet's mind, and is here being recalled (by Jeremiah or the anthologist) with Judah in mind.

30:12-17   Here old complaints are recalled and answered. Every line of verses 12-15 recalls a question or a protest voiced early in Jeremiah's ministry (15:18; 14:19; 8:22; 22:20, 22; 8:16; 6:23). Querulous objections raised long ago against his warnings still smart in the prophet's memory: " 'Your wound is incurable,' you say"; " 'No balm for your wound' — so you say"; " 'Your guilt is great, the fault is yours,' you keep on saying!" But now the warnings are vindicated, the blow has fallen, and the wounds indeed seem fatal (vv. 12-15).

Yet those who devoured Judah shall be devoured; God, who dealt the blow, will heal the wounds. Israel has no one else to help her! And why should God thus help? *Because God's pride is hurt!* Enemies have dared to call his people outcasts and the holy city a place for which no one cares (vv. 16-17).

Surely a novel ground of hope — to save God's face!

30:18-22   Comment must not spoil this perfect lyric, lucid as it stands. But note how it embraces the homes of ordinary people ("tents") and the palace; songs, family life, children in the streets, a congregation in the temple, civic security; a native ruler, enjoying God's favor (as a priest?), set over a liberated people (not, like recent kings, appointed by foreign overlords), and a new Jerusalem.

Nostalgia and hope have kissed each other! What more could Judah ask? Plainly, the people are here in exile, but the date cannot be very late, for no one acquainted with post-exilic Jerusalem could have written so (see 31:1-6).

30:23-24 = 23:19-20 This passage is perhaps repeated here for the sake of its last line. But perhaps the reference in 23:19-20 to God's anger against Judah (which false prophets could not understand) is here used of God's anger against Babylon, which again Judah will come to understand "afterward."

31:1-6 Verses 4-6 recall the lyric quality of 30:18-22, and promise for the countryside what the former poem promised for the city: the restoration of the old, carefree, happy life and its health-giving occupations. Here again the northern kingdom seems especially in view, and its unity with Judah is to be fully restored after the manner of Josiah's centralization of worship (v. 6) and in oneness of spirit.

That much is clear. But verses 2-3 defeat translation. The RSV (ignoring "the sword" in v. 2) makes the lines recall the exodus, to suggest that the same divine faithfulness will see Israel safely home from exile. The NIV makes of verse 2 a promise to survivors of the fall of Jerusalem, and the beginning of verse 3 a curious reference to "the past." With its customary smoothness, the NEB paraphrases as follows: "A people that survived the sword found favor in the wilderness; Israel journeyed to find rest; long ago the Lord appeared to them: I have dearly loved you from of old, and still I maintain my unfailing care for you."

This last is probably close to the poet's intention, to present a new argument for hope: the "everlasting love" that through all the defeats, disasters, suffering, and frustrations of the long centuries has remained faithful to Israel. Even now, with the land devastated and the people in exile, that love will not let them go. City and countryside will yet be happy once more. Long-established vineyards imply security of tenure; lonely Jeremiah can still appreciate communal rejoicing and celebrations — and dancing maidens (vv. 1-6).

This is another idyllic picture, very different from the situation faced by Haggai and Nehemiah on the return from exile; further, the promise to Samaria (v. 5) would sound very strange amid the hostilities of the post-exilic years. No reason, then, to deny the poem to Jeremiah: it is prophecy, not contemporary history.

31:7-14 The journey home! God calls neighboring nations to watch the cavalcade of the returning exiles — a daring exercise of exultant imagination. Bold, too, are the description of Israel as "chief" (RSV), "foremost" (NIV) among the nations, and the call to the watchers to advertise as far as the distant coastlands God's great goodness in regathering Israel, as once they had proclaimed how dreadfully he had scattered them. Like 30:18-22 and 31:1-6, the description of Israel's homecoming reaches the height of lyrical poetry, worthy of being compared with Isaiah 35 and 40 on the same theme. (In v. 7 the NIV has "Lord, save" = "hosanna"; v. 14 serves as a reminder that Jeremiah was a priest, and sometimes hungry.)

As to date: No one who witnessed the slow return of broken groups in post-exilic years could have written in this exalted way. Even in the later years of exile, the people had to be *persuaded* to make the journey home, as in later chapters of the book of Isaiah. "Bring," "from the north country," "return here," and "come" (vv. 8, 9, 12) presuppose that the poem is written in Judah. A new reason is given for the people's redemption: God is father to Israel, Ephraim his favorite firstborn. The old relationship holds.

31:15-20 This poem also speaks as from within Palestine, though the people have gone. The northern kingdom ("Ephraim") seems exclusively in view. Rachel, mother of Joseph and Benjamin, tribal ancestress of Ephraim and Manasseh, weeps within her tomb for her children passing into exile (see "Female Bit-Parts," in Chapter Four of this volume, p. 46). Some think that the words are an old folk-lament; others, that the poem was suggested when Jeremiah was at Ramah after the city fell, and while the new hope of return was fresh in his mind (v. 15; cf. 40:1).

But the time for tears is over: Rachel's children shall return. Meanwhile, God has heard Ephraim lamenting like a prodigal son in a far country, and God's heart is moved as for a "darling child" long absent. God's yearning is explanation enough why the exiled shall return (vv. 16-20).

31:21-22 This obscure fragment appears to appeal to Israel to *enter* the Exile in the firm faith that she will return, so setting up guideposts (or, more probably, noting landmarks) by which she shall find her way back. Israel seems hesitant; she must make up her mind that she *will* return eventually. The last line — "For the Lord has created a new thing on the earth: a woman protects a man" — is a conundrum. Immense cleverness has kindled no conviction of its meaning; the clue is lost. Isaiah also speaks of God's performing some unheard-of wonder to assist the return of the exiles (Isa. 43:19; 40:4). If that provides any hint of what Jeremiah meant, then the Hebrew text had suffered badly even before the Greek version ("men shall go about in safety") was made.

31:23-26 In this fragment the prophet is carried forward to days when, despite the present devastation of city and countryside, there shall again be a time when tillers of the soil and leaders of flocks move over the landscape (of Judah, in this instance), when the weary shall find quiet refreshment and the faint discover new strength. Then people shall once more bless

the temple as the home of righteousness and Zion as God's holy
hill.

A pleasant dream? Yes, as yet, but prophetic.

The New Covenant

31:27-30 This is an oracle recalling the terms of Jeremiah's
call: the plucking up and breaking down having certainly been
fulfilled, the building and planting should begin (cf. 1:10).
Again God promises a springtime ("almond-blossom time") to
sow the empty land again with "the seed of man and the seed
of beast" (v. 27). And he who at the prophet's call had watched
over Judah's sins will watch now as faithfully over her fresh
start. One can almost hear the prophet asking himself how his
new message of hope accords with the terms of his original
commission!

But fulfillment is still to come and in one respect will
be revolutionary. Hitherto, the deep assumption of Hebrew
religion had been a *corporate* relationship between God and
his "people," the family-nation. Within that blood-related
community, the individual had found his status, duty, destiny,
and responsibility — and, too often, his doom also. God was
seen to visit the iniquity of the fathers upon their children,
even to four generations. As the proverb expressed it, the
fathers ate sour grapes, but it was the children's teeth that
were set on edge. Divine justice was corporate, too (Lam. 5:7).
In the ruin of Jerusalem and the Exile that must follow, many
would suffer who in their private lives had not deserved such
punishment.

Jeremiah's whole experience and thought challenged this
assumption as an *incomplete* conception of the relation between
humankind and God. Throughout his ministry he had
struggled, in ever deeper loneliness, with an individual protest

against merely communal and inherited conceptions of duty and destiny. His had almost always been a *lone* voice. And alone with God, he had argued repeatedly about God's treatment of him, an individual, driven by his own conscience, his hand against every man's, to oppose the community around him.

So, in the closing words of this brief oracle, Jeremiah formulates a radically new thought: No longer shall one generation blame another for its sufferings; all shall bear their own individual responsibility. That truth must be held *alongside* the corporate conception of religion as a complement to it. This insight marked an important turning-point, not only in biblical thought but also in the long history of religion.

Ezekiel borrowed his master's text to preach his own vigorous sermon on the individual's accountability to God (Ezek. 18), living as he did in the midst of exiles eager to blame everyone but themselves for their plight. Doubtless Jeremiah faced the beginning of this face-saving attitude in the later days of the siege and afterward, and foresaw the importance, for Judah's future spiritual welfare, of clear self-understanding and an undisguised acceptance of responsibility. What more was needed, the next passage shows.

31:31-34 Besides acknowledged responsibility for sin and tragedy (see the foregoing), any rebirth of Judah would also require a new relation to God. This promise of a *new* covenant between God and humankind, replacing that which Israel had repeatedly broken, is one of the most important paragraphs in the Old Testament, one of the most central to biblical religion.

It is therefore one of the most debated passages as to date and authorship, though competent judges are prepared to say that there are no insuperable objections to the prophecy's authenticity and no rival claimants to its authorship. The compiler(s) of the anthology of hope obviously believed the passage to be Jeremiah's. Ezekiel's clear echoing of it (Ezek. 37:26; 36:24-28) tends to confirm that belief almost in Jeremiah's own time. And Jeremiah's insistence — from his earliest ministry to the end — on the seriousness of Judah's breaches of the ancient covenant led almost inevitably to just such a prophecy, if Judah was to know restoration.

As we have seen, Israel's relation to her God was covenantal and voluntary, not "natural" or "ancestral" — a conception unique to Israel in the ancient world and a major theme of Jeremiah's ministry (see the commentary on 18:1-17, pp. 62-64). Any hope of security for Judah in the future must rest upon renewal of that covenantal relationship, but now it must involve an internal, intuitive knowledge of God and of his will (the "heart to know" of 24:7), shared by the least and the greatest in society, without need of mutual instruction. It must include also complete forgiveness of past sins, and its terms must be written within the personality of each, "upon the heart" — not, as later rabbis were to emphasize, on the memory (as known "by heart") but within the self as the center of the individual's will and of life's direction (vv. 33-34).

Such radical revision of the *terms* of the covenant was necessitated by Israel's continued failures. Unchanged, however, was the central *purpose* of the original covenant: that God should be Israel's God and that they should be his people. For the new covenant, like the old, will be made with Israel and Judah: the corporateness of healthy religious experience is to be preserved as clearly as individual faith, responsibility, and blessing.

Time unfolded immense implications from Jeremiah's new conception. A covenant based upon individual knowledge of God and personal obedience to his will must eventually become inter-racial; as Paul was to insist, the covenanting community would no longer be the family-nation descended from Abraham but all, of every race, who share his faith in God. Further, Jeremiah appears to assume that the suffering and humiliation of defeat and exile would of themselves transform the moral and spiritual nature of the covenant people; punishment would change them. Living among the exiles later, Ezekiel found this had not happened, and he introduced into his exposition of Jeremiah's promise of a new covenant three additional elements: a total *cleansing* of motive, feeling, and desire (probably by reaction against surrounding heathen ways); a new "heart of flesh" (responsive feeling) replacing the former obdurate "heart of stone"; and the Spirit of God creating a new spirit within the people to ensure fulfillment of the covenant's terms (Ezek. 36:24-32).

In this wonderful anticipation of the ever-greater mercies of God, master prophet and disciple together bring the faith of the Old Testament to its culminating point and reach forward to the New. (The RSV and the NEB print vv. 31-34 as prose; the NIV, persuasively, prints them as poetry. Hebrews 8:9 quotes v. 32 from the Greek, Syriac versions.)

> *Reflection:* This is the point at which Jeremiah the Indomitable enters the shadowed Upper Room with Jesus on the night on which he was betrayed. By doing so he gives added meaning to the bread and wine of Passover, and added illumination to the waiting cross. By the same token he enters into every celebration of the Christian Eucharist, constantly to renew in every faithful heart the divine covenant of forgiveness, inward renewal, obedience, and immeasurable hope.

31:35-37; 33:14-26 In these two passages, one essential idea is explored, first in poetry, then in prose: namely, that God's actions in relation to his people are as regular, consistent, and dependable as his actions in the ordered universe. Like the fixed order of sun, moon, stars, and sea is the fixed intention of God that Israel shall remain a nation. That God should cast off his people is as unthinkable as that man should measure the universe. In every realm, what God "covenants" stands unchangeable (31:35-37).

So, too, God's covenant with David's line and with the

Levitical priests is as dependable as sunrise and nightfall, their numbers as measureless as stars and sand. In spite of what the nations say, God's relations with "the family" of Israel and "the family" of Judah, and also with David, are as unalterable as day and night, the stars above, and the earth beneath (33:19-26).

Here, surely, some caution is justified. The second version of the argument is, for Jeremiah, prosy and labored. Such sudden concern with David's line and the number of priests is very surprising; 33:14-26 is not in the Greek version (presumably because it is not in its Hebrew original). Moreover, 33:14-16 repeats 23:5-6, where "the Lord is our righteousness" described not Jerusalem but the Messiah; in addition, 31:35 = Isaiah 51:15. Jeremiah's words appear to have been adapted and augmented somewhat in the hands of the collector(s), though doubtless the original thought was his.

And a stimulating thought it is — "natural law paralleled in the spiritual world," the consistency of the divine character manifested alike in Nature and Spirit, matter and mind, creation and redemption, eternity and time.

31:38-40 If further evidence were needed that the anthology of hope consists of utterances originally separate, some dating from after Jerusalem's fall but long before the exiles' return, this brief "surveyor's report" provides it. Nostalgia for *well-remembered* corners of the city's walls and gates prompts hope for reconstruction on a larger scale, with more devoted dedication and more lasting security. Some think that this fragment does not "sound" like Jeremiah, though evidently the compiler(s) thought that at least the idea was his, perhaps because the inclusion of the "unclean" parts of the city — even Hinnom, the site of human sacrifices — within the renewed sacred precinct accords so well with Jeremiah's hope for Judah's complete cleansing and forgiveness.

33:10-13 Here the destruction of Judah and Jerusalem are plainly past, but no one who saw the exiles' return could describe the situation with such eager delight. This is how one would write who saw devastation and longed to see rehabilitation; this is prophecy, not record. The familiar phrases deliberately reverse old warnings (see 7:34; 16:9; 25:10). A new note is glad *worship* — gladness overflowing to Judah's very frontiers. In place of "terror on every side," Jeremiah now anticipates joy in every direction.

A few more fragments concerned with Judah's future occur in later chapters of the book of Jeremiah, but the precious "little book of comfort" ends at 33:26 (see the commentary on 31:35-37). The story of Jerusalem's last days is then resumed. As we have seen, the anthology's visionary descriptions of the exiles' journey home and their resettlement amid idyllic surroundings, a new Israel in a new land under a radically new covenant, are all very different from the actual conditions of the return. Yet they are such as a despairing remnant of the poorest left in the ruined land or newly arrived in Babylon would need to hear if they were to sustain any faith at all in God and the future.

Jeremiah's Optimism

In that vision of the future, one striking feature is the reconciliation expected between Israel and Judah as a direct result of the reconciliation of each with God (recall 30:4; 31:1, 6, 31; etc.). In this hope, the names "Israel" and "Judah" become almost synonymous. Even more striking are the motives affirming *why* God should ever restore this sinful nation:

- the *measured* justice of God's punishments;
- God's pride when spectator nations jibe at Israel as a people unloved;
- the undying favor ("grace") of God;
- God's everlasting love;

- God's fatherly care even for a prodigal people;
- God's unalterable "concern," his "watching" over his people;
- God's invitation to renew covenant with him on revised, more promising terms;
- God's covenant with Israel, as consistent and steadfast as the laws of the universe;
- God's constant willingness to try again, making all things new;
- and — behind all, controlling all, and sustaining all — God's own ultimate purposes for the world.

Such was Jeremiah's optimism. If only for this, the anthology of hope has incomparable and timeless value.

> *Reflection:* God's character, faithfulness, and love — not our need, deserving, or prayers — are *always* our deepest ground for courageous confidence in tomorrow. His unswerving purpose of good is our strongest argument for hope.

10

Anticlimax

It is to be hoped that Jeremiah's dawning vision of the future sustained him during the dreadful years that followed the fall of Jerusalem. With that event, public affairs passed almost completely beyond his influence, and his long, active, controversial ministry petered out in great sadness. Judah had indeed become as Samaria, and the temple as Shiloh. Except for a very brief period before the Roman occupation, Judah would never again be a sovereign state until the twentieth century.

Conditions in Jerusalem are probably described in Lamentations 1. Nebuchadrezzar had learned that forbearance did not pay in dealing with stubborn Jews, and he made sure there would be no more rebellions. A short, moving comment on Judah's fate is preserved later in the book of Jeremiah:

50:6-7 This sad description (the opposite of Psalm 23) likens the nation to a flock abandoned to wander from familiar valleys to wild hills, unable to find their way to the fold again, prey to savage enemies. The fault lies with neglectful shepherds, although those who devour the sheep blame the victims for

sinning against their Lord. The description of God as "their
true habitation" in the RSV is well paraphrased in the NIV as
"their true pasture." Here are the "lost sheep" of the *Old* Testament (see the commentary on 50:17-20, p. 142).

39:1–43:7; 52:1-30 The story of Jerusalem's end is
vividly related in the former passage and again more fully in
the second, an "appendix" to the book of Jeremiah — taken
mainly from 2 Kings 24:18–25:21, 27-30 — to complete
Judah's story rather than Jeremiah's. When the city walls were
breached and Zedekiah was captured, Jeremiah was at first
taken in chains with others to Ramah. There he was released
and allowed to choose whether to be cared for in Babylon or to
remain in Judah (40:1-4).

It is not clear whether Jeremiah was given this choice
because of the Babylonians' knowledge of Jeremiah's supposed
pro-Babylon policy or because they felt a half-superstitious
reverence for a prophet (Babylonians were deeply religious).
Jeremiah appears to have hesitated. The RSV (following the
Syriac version) has Nebuzaradan, the captain of the guard,
saying to Jeremiah, "If you remain, then return to Gedaliah"
(40:5); the NIV offers "However, before Jeremiah turned to go"
(the margin providing "answered" for "turned to go"), with
Nebuzaradan adding, "Go back to Gedaliah."

To retire to Babylon with the promise of being cared for
would be attractive to Jeremiah, but it might appear to confirm
that he had been truly "pro-Babylon" and not simply realistic
in advising surrender. To remain in ruined Judah would mean
further hardship and privation, but that could help to preserve
a nucleus having a claim to possession of the land, ready for
the exiles' return. It would also give support and "countenance"
to Gedaliah, the new governor, a member of the ever-loyal
family of Shaphan, as he set up his rallying point at Mizpah
(northwest of Jerusalem) and undertook to represent the remaining Jews before Nebuchadrezzar. Jeremiah chose to stay

and was dismissed by Nebuzaradan with a present and an allowance (40:1-6).

The Governor Murdered

Everything went wrong. The assassination of Gedaliah was due to the envy felt by princes of the Davidic line, to Ammonite greed for plunder, and (to some extent) to the over-trustful nature of Gedaliah's loyal soul (40:13–41:3). If 52:12 and 41:1 refer to the same year, Gedaliah's regime lasted two months. But so much happened during Gedaliah's reign: officers of the Judean army, in hiding, heard of Gedaliah's appointment and journeyed to swear allegiance; other Jews scattered in Moab, Ammon, and Edom also heard about it and came; a harvest was gathered at Mizpah; and information reached Gedaliah that the king of Ammon had heard about his appointment and was plotting to kill him (40:7-16). For all this, two months seems impossibly short. The figures in 52:28-30 are difficult to reconcile with other sources, but if (as seems probable) the third deportation was caused by the murder of Gedaliah, some four or five years had passed since Jerusalem was destroyed. In that relatively peaceful interval, Jeremiah *may* have had opportunity to think over past and future, and out of that reflection may have been born "the anthology of hope."

The sudden loss of Gedaliah, the persistent violence of the assassin (41:4-15), and fear of Babylonian revenge left the miserable survivors little choice but flight. The old ally Egypt was one obvious refuge. Once again Jeremiah had to undergo the humiliating experience of being consulted, taking time to inquire about God's will, recommending submission and advising trust in Babylon's fairness and in God's protection, and then being wholly ignored — despite the most solemn oath to obey him. It had happened so often! (41:16–43:7).

We can only guess why the opposing counselors should blame Baruch for Jeremiah's advice. There may have been a suspicion that Jeremiah was by this time too aged, weak, and weary to think for himself. Much against their will, prophet and scribe were taken to Egypt. We are surprised to learn that the king's daughters were among this group taken into exile, but since Zedekiah was only thirty-two when Jerusalem fell, the princesses were probably very young when committed to Gedaliah's care (41:10).

Back to Egypt

So, except for the exiles in Babylon (Jeremiah's "good figs"), the long story of Israel ended where it began — in Egypt. Jeremiah experienced yet another change of circumstance: from prisoner in Jerusalem, to privileged captive, to governor's adviser, to friendless prisoner of the recalcitrant fugitives living in enforced exile. But he had yet two messages to bring, even to that diminutive company of stubborn Jews.

43:8-13 When the fleeing Judahites reached Egypt's frontier at Tahpanhes and awaited permission to enter, Jeremiah was deeply aware of the tragic moment: of a direct denial of all his anti-Egyptian policy through the years; of the dramatic reversal of the historic exodus with which Israel's nationhood began; and of the fatal breach of the covenant then made with God. It was a moment for memorable speech. Instead, Jeremiah was commanded to act, but with unmistakable meaning.

Solemnly, before the Pharaoh's royal lodge in this military town, with a deputation of Jews looking on, Jeremiah laid great stones that were to be the foundation for the throne and royal pavilion which *Nebuchadrezzar* would erect, from which he would exercise judgment upon Egypt. The details are obscure, and it is difficult to imagine the old man being allowed to dig

in the brick pavement or to make mortar (RSV; "clay," NIV).
Some ancient versions have "bury in secret" (does the RSV's
"hide" refer to activity done at night?). Since Jeremiah often
received his inspiration by perceiving meanings in scenes at
hand, we might guess that repairs or extensions were already
being made, prompting the message and providing the materials for a symbolic act that would help toward its own fulfillment.

The long arm of Nebuchadrezzar would reach the Jews
even in Egypt. He would burn Egypt's temples, capture her
gods, wrap himself round with Egypt as a shepherd dons his
cloak (NIV; or "roll up Egypt as a shepherd rolls his cloak" —
to carry it away?; the RSV's "shall clean the land of Egypt, as a
shepherd cleans his cloak of vermin" follows the Greek version).
And he will break down the famous avenue of obelisks before
the temple of the sun at Heliopolis ("city of the sun") and burn
the temples there. When he is ready, Nebuchadrezzar will leave
Egypt, unhampered and unscathed.

There is extra-biblical evidence that a Babylonian invasion
of Egypt occurred in 568 B.C. Obelisks from Heliopolis still
adorn European capitals, including London. But, as always, the
precise details of these predictions were not the point.
Jeremiah's meaning was more general and more solemn: *no*
flight can ever carry one beyond the judgments of God.

Jeremiah's Last Words

44:1-30 The Jewish refugees were becoming widely scattered
in Egypt. That Jeremiah could "address" them presupposes some
representative gathering, perhaps in each district (v. 15). The
spiritual declension which Jeremiah describes suggests that some
time has passed since their arrival in Egypt. Jeremiah reviews the
long story that has ended thus; their breaking of God's covenant

was no ignorant mistake, for God had repeatedly sent them instructors. But they had turned deliberately to gods and cults that had no place in their ancient heritage (vv. 1-6; "burn incense" — literally, "offer up in smoke" — probably includes sacrifices). The old betrayal is still re-enacted. Had Judah learned *nothing?* Had the people forgotten how kings and *queens*, they and their *wives* had courted God's anger in the homeland, that they can repeat the old sins here in Egypt? (vv. 7- 14).

The exiles' response is defiant. Men and women together declare their intention to continue to acknowledge the mother goddess, the queen of heaven — essentially a domestic rite of special interest to the women but connived at by their husbands (see 7:17-18). Even more rebellious is the reason they give for this reversion to idolatry. It is not God's anger they fear; rather, they claim that their desertion of the queen of heaven prompted the woes visited upon them. While they worshipped her, they prospered (vv. 15-19).

To this blasphemy Jeremiah offers no real answer. He reiterates his own reading of their situation and of its cause. As always, the most serious consequence of superstitious religion is moral blindness, the misinterpreting of experience. Against such spiritual darkness there is no argument. But Jeremiah adds this dreadful judicial sentence: "Go ahead then, do what you promised! Keep your [idolatrous] vows!" (v. 25, NIV). Only the people must remember that no Jew in Egypt shall ever again invoke God's sacred name. For he is "watching over them," not now for good but for evil (vv. 20-27; recall 1:12).

For these exiles, this is the end. God is henceforth against them until all but a few are destroyed. And the sign to guarantee that this warning is true? Pharaoh will be delivered to his enemies. When that happens, all will surely understand that God is still sovereign on earth and in heaven — yes, the heaven of the "queen of heaven"! (vv. 28-30; Hophra was deposed about 570 B.C., probably killed in 564 B.C.).

There history leaves Jeremiah, and legend takes over. The most probable account of his end says that he was stoned by his own people (see Heb. 11:37). Tragedy still mingles with heroism, faithfulness with rejection. His last recorded speech echoes words spoken long before to Hananiah (28:9), expressing the true prophet's final argument, the appeal to the vindication of time and the event: "All the remnant of Judah . . . shall know whose word will stand, mine or theirs" (v. 28).

> *Reflection:* The supreme reward authoritatively promised to the true servant of God is not success but "Well done, good and faithful servant! You have been faithful . . ."; the ultimate punishment for rejecting truth is blindness: "If . . . the light within you is darkness, how great is that darkness!" (Matt. 25:21, 23; 6:23, NIV).

11

What about Babylon?

Apart from the "appendix" (chap. 52), the book of Jeremiah closes with a collection of prophecies concerning Babylon (chaps. 50-51), which raises certain problems. That Jeremiah should have much to say concerning a powerful neighbor so closely involved with Judah's fate is hardly surprising. But 50:1 reveals that someone else is telling us what Jeremiah "the prophet" said about Babylon. Some passages plainly presuppose varying dates; most assume that Jerusalem is destroyed; but 51:59-64 belongs to the fourth year of Zedekiah. Changes of form (poetry or prose) and of subject (within the main theme) as well as the recurrent headings ("thus says the Lord," etc.) all confirm that here again we have a collection of what Jeremiah said on different occasions, put together (presumably) by whoever wrote 50:1. The date of collection, rather than of utterance, is therefore reflected in some expressions. The interest of the whole is now *mainly* historical.

Israel Vindicated

Although Babylon's fate is the main theme, a few verses are concerned chiefly with Israel and Judah:

50:4-5 This is a moving description, entirely within Jeremiah's style and thought, written as from within Palestine (indicated by v. 4, and the Hebrew of v. 5), of Israel and Judah reunited and penitent, seeking the way homeward to Zion, to renew their broken covenant with God.

50:17-20 This appears to be a second treatment of the idea in 50:6-7 (see the commentary on these verses in the previous chapter, pp. 134-35). But here the marauding lions are foremost, and their punishment is announced. God will restore Israel to its own pasture; the areas named belonged to the north, though Israel's iniquity *and* Judah's sin shall no longer be found but be forgiven.

50:33-34 These lines contrast the strength of those who hold Israel and Judah captive with the greater strength of Israel's redeemer. The comparison is for Israel a ground of rest, but for Babylon one of unease. There is no doubt of the outcome of *that* contest! It is remarkable that here Israel and Judah suffer one captivity, though a hundred years apart.

51:34-40 This passage has more on Babylon's future: it describes God wreaking vengeance on the beautiful city, drying up her famous protective moats, creating a wasteland haunted by wild beasts, a deserted wilderness. After their excitement, feasting, drunkenness, and noisy laughter (NIV), Israel's conquerors shall fall into a drunken stupor and never wake. At this point they are ready to be sacrificed.

All this is to defend Israel's "cause," for she has been devoured, emptied (like a jar), swallowed up, and then vomited forth (NIV). Defense of a cause suggests a complaint laid before the emperor, who is too drunk to attend to it, but the figure of a gluttonous meal has obscured this. Babylon has "made a meal" of Israel; in return, God shall make a feast of Babylon (vv. 34, 39-40). (Verses 34 and 44 may well have supplied the seed-thought for the brilliant story of the book of Jonah.)

Babylon's Future

The remaining poems, prophecies, and comments in chapters 50 and 51 concern Babylon herself. Since very few clues are given about their date or occasion, rearrangement under themes involves no loss, and it serves to relieve tedious repetition and to suggest the progress of *events* rather than the development of the prophet's thought. Babylon's fall is announced (in five items), the enemy is called to arms (in four items), a battle begins (mentioned in three items), and the end is twice described. Of course, details overlap widely: Babylon's coming desolation is referred to eleven times; her capture and destruction, nine times; and Israel's flight from Babylon, seven times.

51:20-23 A powerful single stanza describes Babylon as God's "battle-hammer," or "war club." This mace, or "maul," was favored by Assyrians and adopted by Babylon (cf. 50:23). God is supreme, and uses nations as he wills; Jeremiah three times names Nebuchadrezzar as God's servant (25:9; 27:6; 43:10), and Nebuzaradan, the captain of the guard, makes a similar claim (40:2-3). It is an unexpected conception for a Jewish mind.

50:35-38 This forceful malediction has the form of a curse (cf. 51:59-64): "[May] a sword [be] upon . . ." ("against," NIV) — though the curt ejaculation is stronger. (In v. 36, the RSV's "diviners" is nearer Babylonian thought than the NIV's "false prophets." In v. 38, the RSV's "drought" slightly alters the Hebrew for "sword," a copyist thinking that a sword upon *waters* was inappropriate. The literal translation of the last line of v. 38 — "With terrors they make themselves mad" — is hardly the equivalent of the NIV's "idols that will go mad with terror," since Jews denied idols any consciousness; the RSV offers "they are mad over idols"; the NEB neatly contrives "a land of idols that glories in its dreaded gods." The main point is clear: a superstitious curse is being pronounced upon a superstitious people.)

God's Hostility toward Babylon

51:25-26 With God against, who can defend? The figure of a volcano scattering fire far and wide until it burns itself out in a desolate wasteland, leaving soft, cooled lava of no use for rebuilding, would be all too familiar in the Dead Sea region, though inappropriate to Babylon's plains. It excellently describes a dying empire, once destroying all rivals but now burned out, crumbling, and ready (in an earthquake?) to be leveled to a flat plain.

51:15-19; 10:1-16 Israel's God, maker and Lord of Nature, is far superior in might to the foolish images that ignorant men worship. These "gods" are simply helpless in days of distress. So very different is "the portion of Jacob," the chosen Lord, he who made all things, the Lord almighty. Omnipotence confronts mere impotence! This forthright challenge is appropriate to its present position, but it is part of the longer poem of 10:1-16, which interrupts its context and betrays its late date by condemning elaborate idol-manufacture and gorgeous images instead of the pagan manifestations of Jehoiakim's reign: Canaanite fertility cults, worship of the queen of heaven, sun worship, and the wooden pillars of Ashtar (cf. Isa. 40:18-20 and 44:9-20 from exilic times).

The poem's opening lines (10:1-10) warn the people of Israel against imitating the paganism around them in Babylon, with its fear of eclipses and comets, its practice of astrology, and its great skill in god-making. Such manufactured gods cannot speak ("like a scarecrow in a melon patch," NIV); "they have to be carried," and can do neither harm nor good. For all their cost, artistry, and fancy dress, they cannot be compared with the true and living God, unsurpassed in all the world, whose anger makes the very earth tremble.

At 10:11, Aramaic expressions interrupting verses 10-12 betray a marginal comment by a copyist. Verses 12-16 = 51:15-19, addressed now to Babylon, who more than any other nation had cause to fear the might of the living God despite her hosts of idols. It is easy to discern allusions to Babylon's reputation for astrology, for science, and for the magnificence of her temples. But what hope has idolatrous Babylon in contest with the living God?

The reasons for God's hostility toward Babylon are made very clear:

50:28 Babylon has affronted God himself. Listen to the escaping exiles making their way home to Zion to declare God's vengeance for what was done to his temple!

51:11 This verse similarly declares that God is stirring up the Medes to overthrow Babylon because of her desecration of his temple.

51:24 Another mere fragment names "all the evil that they have done in Zion" as the reason for God's hostility.

51:49 This verse is succinct: "Babylon must fall for the slain of Israel, [just] as for Babylon have fallen the slain of all the earth."

51:56 This verse adds a deeper reason for vengeance: "the Lord is a God of recompense, he will surely requite."

That is to say, God opposes Babylon for both religious and humanitarian reasons, because his own character is unalterably just. Jeremiah leaves side by side the two assertions: that Babylon is God's servant in the punishment of Judah (see the commentary on 51:20-23, p. 143), and that God will punish Babylon for her idolatry, blasphemy, and inhumanity. He saw no inconsistency in God's using the wrath of man for his own purposes without excusing that cruelty (contrast Hab. 1:12-13).

Babylon Will Fall

50:11-13   This passage is addressed *to* Babylon; contrast it with verses 14-16. It announces her coming disgrace and desolation despite her exultant plundering of Judah. Once the greatest among nations, she will become least, and those who once praised her, standing in awe, will scoff at her downfall. For God is angry.

50:31-32   God being against Babylon and her day for punishment having come, all her pride cannot save her, nor any dare to help her. All is doomed to burn: the Lord says so.

50:39-40   Henceforth only wild things shall dwell in Babylon, as in the cities beside the Dead Sea. Translators have difficulty here with rare, uncertain words: should it be "wild beasts" or "marmots"; "jackals," "hyenas," or "wolves"; "ostriches" or "owls"? Also unclear is whether the prophecy is in prose or poetry. But the utter, permanent desolation of the ancient city is made very certain.

51:41-53   Hebrew tenses, always uncertain, here confuse past, "prophetic perfect," and future, though either literary form declares the certain future. "Sheshach" (v. 41, NIV) is a code name for Babylon, which other nations once called "the praise of the whole earth," which stands in sharp contrast with the horror they are about to witness. The tidal wave (v. 42) may symbolize war.

The god Bel shall yield up all that he has swallowed and shall no longer feed on men. Even Babylon's immense city wall — Herodotus says it was 75 feet wide and 300 feet high! —

will crumble at last. (Darius the Mede eventually destroyed it.) God's people, forewarned by rumors, must leave the city without fear, for the time is appointed for Babylon's humiliation before heaven and earth. Her destroyers will approach from the north; the picture grows steadily clearer. (Verse 49 is an epigram of simple historical justice.)

The same justice shall vindicate Judah. Called to remember God and Jerusalem from this distant, stricken city and to be prepared to leave, Judah replies that she is ashamed that aliens ever violated the sacred courts of Zion. God answers that in return he will punish the idols of Babylon till the groans of her wounded fill the land (in place of the ecstatic cries of idol worshipers?). These things *will* happen, though Babylon build her wall to the very heavens.

51:58 Babylon's famous wall is mentioned yet again (see the foregoing) to remove any doubt whether a city so strongly fortified could ever be overcome. This verse appears to imply that foreign labor erected it, and all for nothing in the end.

Call to Arms

50:8-10 Certain of those among Babylon's captives (surely the Jews) are urged to take the lead in leaving Babylon, like "he-goats before the flock." In the north a conspiracy of nations is already stirring. They shall "array themselves against" Babylon; every arrow shall find its mark, and they shall plunder until they are sated.

50:14-16 The attacking armies are here called to take up position around Babylon. Hardly are the first arrows loosed and the war cry sounded than her defenses begin to crumble, for God is in this! Let the invaders requite Babylon's own behavior with just vengeance, starving the city by isolating her from the countryside and its produce. So shall all her captives (foreign workers? conscripts? mercenaries?) be free to desert and return to their homes.

50:29-30 Again archers are called to encircle Babylon, letting no one escape. She must be treated as she treated others, she who defied even "the Holy One of Israel." So shall her warriors fall hemmed within the city, never reaching the open field. (In chap. 49, v. 26, the equivalent of v. 30, is spoken to Damascus.)

50:41-46 Whether rendered in one poem (NIV) or in both poetry and prose (vv. 41-43 in poetry, vv. 44-46 in prose, RSV), the thought is connected: it presents a vivid picture of an army, with many kings, mustering from the north. The future grows still clearer. Their ruthless character, their military might (warriors armed with bows and spears, though the NEB has "sabres"), and their horses (in Jewish eyes the last word in war preparation) all threaten *total* disaster. Hence the helpless terror of the king of Babylon.

This overwhelming attack is likened to a lion venturing from Jordan's thick woodlands to the upland pastures to attack a flock. The "lion" is not here named, but God is planning all. No "shepherd" (ruler) can withstand such fierceness; the "flock" (Babylon) will surely be carried off, and all who hear of it shall tremble at the danger. (The passage is composite: vv. 41-43 = 6:22-24, where it concerns the Scythians; vv. 44-46 resemble the message to Edom in 49:19-21. Varying modern translations show how obscure is the Hebrew text.)

"Let Battle Commence!"

51:1-14 Babylon's destruction is God's judgment, but through human agents. "Spirit" in verse 1 also means the "wind" that "winnows" in verse 2 (hence "a destroying wind" in the RV and the NEB). A great army will toss Babylon into the air to be blown away, leaving the land windswept. ("Leb Kamai" [NIV] or "Qamai" is another code word for Babylon.) Let the attack be so swift as to catch the defenders unprepared; the pick of the army shall die within the city. (Verse 5 seems to combine Babylon's and Israel's guilt, obscurely, as modern translations show; probably it provides two reasons for confident attack: God is *for* Israel and *against* Babylon.)

A fascinating dialogue follows among onlookers watching the attack. Captives or mercenaries urge flight to escape Babylon's fate. Others comment (wistfully, or in fairness?) upon Babylon's past power, now justly repaid by the madness of those she made drunk. A third voice calls (ironically?) for sympathy, wondering if she can be healed. Yet others (or the first group again) declare her judgment beyond cure, and repeat the advice to go, "each to his own country." To this, Judah replies, "The Lord has brought forth our vindication; come, let us declare in Zion the work of the Lord our God" (v. 10).

The poet takes up again the call to attack, naming the rebel province — Media. Behind her is God's decree, organizing vengeance. Display the war banner, strengthen the guard, prepare ambushes! Neither her waterways nor her wealth shall save Babylon. God has taken an oath, and men, "as many as locusts" (v. 14), swarm to accomplish his will: their triumph is assured. (If the RSV is right in making v. 11 prose, it may be a later comment, naming the enemy; v. 13 contains a weaving metaphor — "the thread of your life is cut.")

51:27-33 "Prepare the nations for war against Babylon" with standard, trumpet, summons, marshals, horses, the backing of local rulers, and armies whose marching shakes the very earth. For God's purpose against Babylon stands firm! And already Babylon's defenders, panic-stricken, cease fighting; houses burn; the bars of her great gates are breaking. A dispatch runner from one side of the city meets another from the other side; each reports heavy assault. The water barriers are crossed, the fortifications on fire, the defenders terrified. The great city has become God's threshing floor, where the harvest which Babylon has so long sown and now reaps is being trodden out. (In v. 32, for the NIV's odd "the *marshes* set on fire," the NEB has "the guard-towers set on fire.")

Several of these expressions have occurred already, but here the picture is greatly sharpened. Whole governments are involved; subkingdoms in northern Armenia are supporting the effort (v. 27); the city is completely surrounded. Can all this be prevision? imaginative prediction? or well-informed hindsight? Perhaps, more probably, it is prevision preserved and edited with hindsight.

50:21-27 Two puns introduce this further description of the battle of Babylon. A word meaning "southern Babylonia" is slightly changed to mean "doubly rebellious," and the name of a Babylonian clan is similarly changed to mean "visitation" or "punishment." God orders destruction of "the hammer of the whole earth" (v. 23; recall 51:20-23). Because it strove against him, a whole empire is caught in God's snare. God has work to do in Babylonia, and he has armed himself in readiness.

So the command is given: Open up Babylon like a granary, and heap her up like grain; she is being harvested. Slaughter her "young bulls" (NIV; that is, kill the younger warriors, leaving her defenseless in the future). For Babylon's end is near. In verse 26, "destroy her utterly" (RSV) means literally "devote utterly to God in sacrifice," and implies a holocaust of stored foodstuffs, treasures, animal stock, and the bodies of soldiers, ablaze in the city squares, a colossal sacrifice.

The End of Babylon

50:1-3 This is the clearest declaration, to all peoples, that Babylon has fallen. If her chief gods — Bel and Merodach (Marduk) — and her many idols could not save her, what hope remains for other heathen peoples? God is not mentioned; the facts speak for themselves. The NIV translates the verses as prediction (as the vagueness of Hebrew tenses permits), but alien nations would not be impressed by a Jewish prophet's asserting his hope as the word of his God. The terms imply a wide proclamation of what *has* happened.

51:54-57 The "noise of great destruction" and the shrill cries of warriors drown the "mighty voice" of the great city, as God lays Babylon waste. The "God of recompense" will repay in full. It remains for Babylon's rulers, commanders, and warriors to drink the cup God holds out to them, then "sleep a perpetual sleep" (cf. 25:15-29, noting there v. 26). The last word rests, as always, with THE King, the Lord of hosts.

Arranged in this way, the "Babylon Collection" provides a vivid, detailed, and remarkably well-informed description of the fate of Babylon, from its announcement to its consummation. We do not meet elsewhere in the book of Jeremiah this degree of "second sight" prediction, though of course Jeremiah could have been granted prevision even of such details, if need arose. But it is difficult to find appropriate place or purpose for these prophecies within Jeremiah's lifetime.

That Babylon would ultimately fall before God's judgment might encourage Jerusalem's defenders during the siege or the exiles already in captivity, but at that time Jeremiah was counseling surrender, not encouraging resistance, and advising the exiles to settle peaceably. For the exiles in Egypt a little later, the fate of Babylon was largely irrelevant, and Jeremiah's message was rather that Nebuchadrezzar would eventually occupy Egypt.

Fifty years later, toward the closing years of the Exile, these prophecies would have great significance for the generation of exiles born in Babylon. Passages that closely parallel these passages in thought and expression may be found in the later chapters of the book of Isaiah, which are generally thought to be from the pen of one personally acquainted with the situation in those years. Inevitably, therefore, the question arises whether later disciples who saw the events here so minutely described have elaborated and supplemented their master's teaching on Babylon's future.

As we have seen, one *possible* explanation of 51:59-64 is that Jeremiah permitted some friends to share privately his encouraging vision of Babylon's ultimate fate, without thereby compromising his public counsel of surrender. Jeremiah's faith in God's righteousness, in his everlasting love, and in his covenant with Israel required that at some time Babylon should be judged. His belief that Israel still possessed a future and a hope likewise implied that Babylon's power must sooner or later be broken. With such insights to guide them, followers of Jeremiah who treasured his message, and who knew from their own experience in what forms and to what extent his teaching had been vindicated, may well have left us this testimony to Jeremiah's foresight.

But whether or not that is what happened is something each reader of chapters 50-51 will decide, according to his or her own understanding of Hebrew prophecy.

12

A Prophet's Inner Life

One might assume that a prophet's inner life would glow constantly with divine certainty and would be sustained by continually renewed inspiration and self-approval. Jeremiah's experience, however, was far different. Behind his public ministry lay a private life of exceptional intensity — painful, disappointing, and frequently unsure. Outwardly indomitable, he was inwardly hypersensitive and self-questioning. There were many reasons for this.

A priest rejected by other priests, a prophet contradicted by other prophets, Jeremiah carried a double burden. Priests were naturally conservative and traditionalist; prophets were naturally critical and innovative, challenging accepted ideas as no longer relevant. Trying to be both would necessarily generate deep tensions. Similarly, Jeremiah was a patriot, a man who deeply loved his land and his people, but he was condemned to live in an age when the highest patriotism lay in warning of catastrophe, insisting upon surrender of the land, and blaming the people he loved.

Faith and Realism

Jeremiah's faith was nurtured in priestly worship and feeling but was informed with a prophet's sense of the supreme justice of God for himself, for his society, and for all peoples. Perhaps his deepest conviction was that whatever God said "would stand." That faith was to him intimately personal, as his sense of calling and his inability to refuse it illustrate. His exceedingly frank prayers attest to it as well. And he found a personal, divine consolation: "O Lord, my strength and my stronghold, my refuge in the day of trouble. . . . Blessed is the man who trusts in the Lord, whose trust *is* the Lord. He is like a tree planted by water, that sends out its roots by the stream, and does not fear when heat comes, for its leaves remain green, and is not anxious in the year of drought, for it does not cease to bear fruit" (16:19; 17:7-8, emphasis mine).

And yet, Jeremiah was a most uncompromising realist. He saw humankind without illusions: "My people are foolish . . . ; they are stupid children. . . . They are skilled in doing evil, but how to do good they know not. . . . They have rejected the word of the Lord, and what wisdom is in them?" (4:22; 8:9). If the sorry condition of Judah was mainly due to the faithless incompetence of her leaders, the mass of the people "loved to have it so" (5:30-31). Jeremiah thought the human heart the most deceitful of all things, beyond understanding and "beyond cure" (17:9, NIV). "I know, O Lord, that the way of man is not in himself, that it is not in man who walks to direct his steps" (10:23).

That same realism saw clearly that what priests most valued — shrines, rites, sacrifices, symbols, the Ark, the sacred book — could no more safeguard true religion than could a good king's decree. Nor could treasured ancient promises about the security of Jerusalem change the brutal facts of invasion by a powerful foe, since the situation and Judah herself had so greatly changed since the promises were made. Jeremiah read the lesson of Shiloh, and the "empty" land of Israel stretching northward, with unflinching honesty. Most courageous of all was his realistic assessment of his own mission: any attempt to change the character of Judah at this late hour was hopeless; he could only prepare the people for the Exile, which *could* change them.

Such faith and such realism make contentious companions within any sensitive soul.

Piety and Politics

Jeremiah's public life, too, bridged something of a contradiction. As a priest, his concern was religious — opposing the Canaanite cults, supporting the king's reform, calling for renewal of Judah's covenant with God. As a prophet, he spoke always as being sent and instructed by God. In the public mind, Jeremiah was clearly "a religious": that was his protection against assassination.

Yet Jeremiah was at least equally concerned with politics and the social order. In summarizing his teaching, we shall find far more about social righteousness than is commonly associated with Jeremiah. Throughout his ministry, he was occupied with kings, princes, counselors, policies, and parties, and with his nation's place among surrounding peoples. It was his political significance that offended the princes, and he read the political climate for other nations as accurately as for his own.

No one could accuse Jeremiah of seeking political power. But there was much that was secular, down-to-earth, about his religious calling, and something deeply religious about his political counsel — another exceedingly testing role to play! But Jeremiah's inner tensions went deeper yet.

The Knowledge of God

For Jeremiah, the *evidence* of true religion lay in the practice of justice, truth, and mercy; its *essence* he defines, again and again, as "knowing God." This expression becomes in Jeremiah's hands astonishingly rich and fruitful. Negatively, most of the ills which the people suffer and the evils that they do Jeremiah traces to the lack of the knowledge of God (for examples, see 2:8; 4:22; 9:3-6). Positively, Jeremiah's words to Jehoiakim are definitive: "Did not your father eat and drink [i.e., wasn't he content with simple living?] and do justice and righteousness? Then it was well with him. He judged the cause of the poor and needy; then it was well. Is not this to know me?" (22:15-16).

What then is this all-important knowledge of God? In part, it is knowledge of God's law ("requirements," NIV), the "way" that men should "walk" before him (5:4-5). Such requirements are as the homing instincts of the human heart seeking its maker; alas, stork, turtledove, swallow, and crane obey the time of their migration according to a "way" implanted within their nature, but "my people know not" what God has "ordained" for human welfare (see 8:7, RSV). In 16:21, to know God is to know his *power* (literally, his "hand") in one's experience; his *might* (what he can accomplish); and his *name* (his real character) as "the Lord," above all enemies, difficulties, and fears (cf. 24:7).

This, to Jeremiah, is life's supreme aim or "value": " 'Let not the wise man boast of his wisdom or the strong man boast of his strength or the rich man boast of his riches, but let him who boasts boast about this: that he understands and knows me, that I am the Lord, who exercises kindness, justice and righteousness on earth, for in these I delight,' declares the Lord" (9:23-24, NIV). And to know God and the things God delights in is the supreme blessing of the new covenant: "No longer shall each man teach his neighbor and each his brother, saying, 'Know the Lord,' for they shall all know me, from the least of them to the greatest, says the Lord" (31:34).

As a priest, Jeremiah knew that such intimate acquaintance with the living God was never cheaply attained. The knowing is mutual. The whole heart, the life, the past, must be open to God's scrutiny. God knows man as no man knows himself: "I the Lord search the mind and try the heart" (17:10); "[The Lord] seest the heart and the mind" (20:12); "[The Lord] triest the heart and the mind" (11:20). And no man can escape him: "Can a man hide himself in secret places so that I cannot see him? says the Lord. Do I not fill heaven and earth? says the Lord" (23:24). So often does the thought recur to Jeremiah. "But thou, O Lord, knowest me; thou seest me, and triest my mind toward thee" (12:3).

There could be no true knowledge of God without this openness of mind and heart toward God in *mutual* understanding. For Jeremiah, the veil of the temple was already rent. Henceforth, while book, temple, and human mediation might all be helpful in initiating and nurturing the religious life, none would be essential. And none would prove of truly *religious* value without that individual integrity, insight, obedience, and love that knits the individual heart to God.

Conversing with God

For Jeremiah, knowing God began in dialogue. In chapter 1 we overhear "the word of the Lord came to me" and "the Lord said to me" nine times, as well as "I said," "I replied," "I answered" (NIV). This dialogue continued in a series of conversations throughout Jeremiah's life, conversations in which complaint, protest, confession, and even challenge were mingled with occasional praise and petition. It must be admitted that the tone of Jeremiah's prayers is often not what we expect from "a man of prayer" — unless we have listened carefully to some of the psalmists.

11:18–12:6 When Jeremiah visited Anathoth and preached reform, he received a hostile reception and narrowly escaped. This moved him to complain to God that the wicked, the treacherous, who talk of God with godless hearts, thrive and have their way. In contrast, God surely knows that Jeremiah is sincere. So he asks that God will separate out the faithless in Judah as a shepherd chooses out sheep for slaughter. (See chaps. 11 and 12 and the commentary on 11:1-23, pp. 67-69; note 11:21 and 12:6; in the present text, 11:18, 20 and 12:1 seem disarranged, though the meaning is clear.)

God's reply to this, Jeremiah's first complaint, is stern. In two proverb-like questions, God demands, "If even that little opposition and disappointment wearies you, tempting you to give up, how will you endure when real persecution starts?" And such persecution lies just ahead, among Jeremiah's kins-folk, who "speak fair words" but plot his downfall (12:5-6). On reflection, Jeremiah realizes that God has indeed delivered him from worse than he, in lamb-like innocence, had foreseen. He pleads that God will let him see justice — vengeance — wreaked on those who seek his life, for has he not committed his whole cause to God?

> *Reflection:* God's answer to a complaining servant is ever likely to be more bracing than consoling. We do not set the terms on which we serve; to be allowed to be of use is privilege enough.

18:18-23 This vigorous protest to God against ill treatment by men follows Jeremiah's announcement that God, the sovereign potter, was shaping a "plan" against Judah. The people replied that they would pursue their own "plans." Jeremiah records God's comment and then tells how they said,

"Come, let's make plans against Jeremiah" (v. 18, NIV), defending Judah's chosen counselors. (Does some local city-planning contention make the language topical?)

Pleading that God will hear him, Jeremiah reverses his former intercession for Judah: let the people have what they have chosen! He acquiesces in God's "plan" for them, and his anger kindles violent maledictions. The fierce words used describe, in fact, the siege of Jerusalem, step by step, though it happened much later than Jeremiah supposed. Is this prophetic foresight? or early record colored by later experience?

Vindictiveness ought not to breed vindictiveness, but it does. Jeremiah had experienced enough ill will to explain his own. Nor can the prophet's personal anguish and rejection be divorced entirely from his identification with God's cause. But he attempts no personal retaliation. Once aroused, such desire for vindication, slipping over so easily into eagerness for revenge, can have no safer outlet than prayer. Jeremiah asks God to deal with the situation; that shows admirable self-restraint.

> *Reflection:* Such prayers, it may be noticed, receive no
> answer. But they relieve and cleanse the heart — which
> is an answer, after all.

17:14-18 Clearly unconnected with its present context, this prayer might have followed any one of Jeremiah's confrontations with his critics. But his arrest and flogging by Irijah seem especially apposite to the terms used, especially the plea for vindication and *healing* (vv. 14, 18; cf. 37:11-15, and 17:15-16 with 37:17). Not wanting to utter the warning given him but compelled by his overwhelming sense of duty, Jeremiah protests that God himself is becoming a terror to him, a most revealing outburst. Knowing God has placed on him weighty and inescapable obligations. (In v. 16, original obscurity and many "corrections" have placed the meaning beyond recovery.)

Reflection: If Jeremiah's closing imprecation — "destroy them with double destruction!" — offends, we should ask ourselves if we have ever been falsely accused, flogged, and imprisoned for speaking God's word. Even to ask that those who have led others to disaster should themselves suffer disaster is but an appeal to divine justice.

Despair?

20:7-13 The change of mood and theme at verse 14 shows verses 7-13 to be self-contained, even if contemporary with the following verses. Inevitably we recall the day and night that Jeremiah spent in the public stocks at the instigation of Pashhur (20:1-3). "I have become a laughingstock all the day; every one mocks me," he laments. "For the word of the Lord has become for me a reproach and derision all day long" (vv. 7-8). He hears the whispered mockery of old — "Terror on every side!" (v. 10). People he knows seek to trap him in speech: "'Denounce him! Let us denounce him!' say all my familiar friends, watching for my fall" (v. 10). Such persistent insult, mockery, and public reproach would deeply wound Jeremiah's sensitive spirit.

During the long, bitterly painful hours of his overnight punishment, he thinks he might give up prophesying, since always he must proclaim violence and destruction. But with the morning, he realizes that will not do. The word given burns in his bones, and he must speak, though people mock his message as panic-mongering. The word exercises its own compulsion: an honest mind cannot be silent.

Even Jeremiah's "familiar friends" begin to desert him, yet among those "friends" surely is the Lord (v. 11). The persecutors will themselves be disgraced, and not for one night only! Jeremiah pleads to see that day, and breaks into a psalm.

What especially shocks us is Jeremiah's forthright accusation: "O Lord, you deceived me . . . ; you overpowered me and prevailed" (v. 7, NIV). The accepted badge of a true prophet was fulfillment of his predictions (Deut. 18:22), but for years, Jeremiah's predictions had not been literally fulfilled. So Jeremiah might well feel that God has let him down.

But worse: it was supposed that God could use the "prophetic frenzy" to mislead the prophet himself. Micaiah alludes to this strange idea in opposing the prophets of Ahab: "the Lord put a lying spirit in the mouth of all these your prophets" (1 Kings 22:19-23). Ezekiel echoes it (Ezek. 14:9). This notion haunts Jeremiah in his deep despondency. Has God, by superior wisdom and power, misused him for some purpose he cannot understand, by making him speak untruth and then leaving him to suffer the consequences? If not, why doesn't the truth carry conviction and vindicate the speaker?

The idea that God might deceive his own servants sits uncomfortably in modern minds, but it would have been very distressing to Jeremiah. It was a desperate moment, a dark night of the soul in which to issue a daring challenge, as Jeremiah in all integrity struggled to understand his own experience. Not for the first time and not for the last, he found the effort to know God costly. As he faced the options left to him — "intolerable to go on, impossible to give up" — he thought his way through to God who "rescues the life of the needy from the hands of the wicked" (v. 13, NIV). We are relieved that with the coming of the dawn — this time, at any rate — Jeremiah could break into song.

> *Reflection:* Prophet and psalmist alike teach us very firmly that the right way to deal with doubt and protest within the soul is to carry them straight to God and *never* let them carry us away from him. God is his own interpreter, and he will make things plain.

20:14-18 This marks the utmost low point of Jeremiah's spiritual experience. It can hardly belong after verse 13; a cry of reveille and a midday alarm (v. 16) could hint at siege conditions and at Jeremiah's long suffering at that time. For the moment, the tide of the spirit has ebbed far with Jeremiah.

The depth of despondency to which even Jeremiah could fall when he did *not* lift his doubt and protest to God (see the commentary on 20:7-13, pp. 160-61) is here violently illustrated. He curses the day of his birth and the man who announced to his father his safe arrival; that man should have strangled him at birth. (Such infanticide was widespread in the ancient world. The reference to the cities of the plain sounds proverbial, meant to invoke a deep and lasting curse.) Jeremiah's near-despair is underlined by a bitter, unanswerable question: "Why was I born to a life like this?" Now God is mentioned, but only as a pitiless judge in former times.

This outburst of angry frustration and despair (it is thought) probably inspired Job's more literary expression of a similar mood (Job 3). It is an experience not confined to Jeremiah in the Old Testament or by any means unknown among Christians. But even in such darkness, Jeremiah's fundamental piety holds: he does not curse God or his parents.

> *Reflection:* In the previous verses Jeremiah faced the
> tragedy of suffering and evil *with* God, and faced up
> to it; here he faces the same suffering and evil *without*
> God and can only curse. To deny God because of suffer-
> ing and evil appears to ease the intellectual problem
> of faith; it leaves the suffering and evil still inexpli-
> cable, *and now unbearable.*

15:10-21 This confused passage evidently marks a second crisis in Jeremiah's vocation as a prophet. It is plainly the climax of all these outbursts from Jeremiah's overburdened heart. The most that can be said of its occasion is that verse 10 closely resembles 20:14, and the dark mood of both passages recalls those months of confinement and menace during the last siege of Jerusalem.

Modern translations vary so widely that it is difficult to believe that they represent the same verses. In any case, verses 13-14, which make no sense here, belong at 17:3-4; this leaves verse 15 as an answer to verse 12, and clarifies much. Verse 18 refers to the dreaded desert mirage that lures travelers to death with the false promise of water. Verses 12 and 20 echo Jeremiah's call (1:18), as verses 10 and 19 confirm it; the call and its attendant promise are being *renewed*. But it is not clear why this was necessary or what Jeremiah is to "return" from (v. 19; "repent," NIV). Are the complaint in verse 18 (cf. 20:7) and the implied abandonment of his calling in verse 19 (cf. 20:9) the "worthless" words he must avoid — words of self-pity?

Jeremiah's last protest is against the endless strife and contention in which his life has been set. Men curse him as the borrower curses the grasping moneylender, as the moneylender curses the defaulting debtor. The NEB (with partial support from the NIV) makes God answer that he will yet deliver Jeremiah "for a good purpose" and bring these enemies to plead before the prophet. Had not God promised to make him as strong as an iron pillar, a bronze wall? Can anyone break northern Assyria's famous metals? This question Jeremiah can only answer with verse 15. (The RSV makes the confusion in the text — which all three translations refer to — no more intelligible, and leaves v. 12 unanswered.)

Jeremiah then begs that in divine forbearance God will not remove him. The sense of imminent peril seems very clear (v. 15). Is Jeremiah actually enduring (or vividly recalling) that miry dungeon? Reminded perhaps by God's question (v. 12), Jeremiah remembers how God's word first "came" to him (v. 16,

NIV), separating him from common pursuits and entertainments (vv. 16-17). Why has it ended in unceasing pain, "incurable" wounding, and a sense of being deceived by God himself? (see the commentary on 20:7-13, pp. 160-61).

So dreadful a question, born of deep disillusion, shows Jeremiah's "iron and brass" near the breaking point. Jeremiah, it must ever be remembered, had no hope of another life in which wrongs would be righted, wounds healed, and faithful service vindicated.

Once more, God's reply is bracing. If Jeremiah will "repent" of this complaining and "return" to his allegiance, he may yet stand and serve before God. If he will utter worthwhile things, he will still be God's spokesman. Then the people will turn to him; he must not conform to them. And he will yet be all that God has promised — a bronze wall invulnerable to assault, an unbending iron pillar. He shall not be overcome; God will be with him; the wicked shall not have their way.

The crisis did pass, and Jeremiah stood firm. But his self-revelation made plain for all time the inward cost of his outward steadfastness. Jeremiah went on with God, but his pain continued, as did his contentions, and his wounds remained inescapable. His ministry was his cross.

> *Reflection:* On the Sea of Galilee one stormy day, the disciples were in the place Jesus had appointed, doing what Jesus had commanded, going where Jesus had sent them. Yet the rowing was difficult; the wind was contrary; the waves were threatening. Nevertheless, Jesus did not exempt them from labor, contention, or danger. Instead, he joined them. (See Mark 6:45-51.)

The Price of Insight

Like Jacob of old, Jeremiah wrestled with God, but for him there never was a break of day. Yet he became, in some true sense, a prince with God. Reluctant to begin prophesying yet finding no release from it, he served with painful devotion the God who made his weakness indomitable. He, too, cried, "My God, my God, why . . . ?" — which is but the evidence of his deep integrity within the darkness of his spirit (see Mark 15:34). He would not let God go.

This might all appear cruel and fruitless if we could not recognize its effects, in later years, *for Israel* as she returned from exile with Jeremiah's interpretation of her tragedy laid forever upon her conscience. And it might appear harsh and pointless if we had not history's long hindsight by which to assess the new understanding of religion that came *to all people* out of Jeremiah's heart-searching, heartbreaking experience. For out of Jeremiah's passion and pain emerged his permanent message for the world, his legacy for humankind.

A devout scholar of a past generation, A. S. Peake, prefaced his painstaking study of the book of Jeremiah with lines from F. W. H. Myers' *St. Paul,* lines he rearranged as a most penetrating comment upon the prophet's inner life:

Nay but much rather let me late returning
     Bruised of my brethren, wounded from within,
Stoop with sad countenance and blushes burning,
     Bitter with weariness and sick with sin . . .

Thus as I weary me and long and languish,
     No wise availing from that pain to part, —
Desperate tides of the whole great world's anguish
     Forced thro' the channels of a single heart, —

So to Thy presence get me and reveal it,
  Nothing ashamed of tears upon Thy feet,
Show the sore wound, and beg Thine hand to heal it,
  Pour Thee the bitter, pray Thee for the sweet.

Then, with a ripple and a radiance thro' me . . .

But in Jeremiah's case the ripple and the radiance of answering blessing was to come very long afterward, and in other lives, other generations, and other lands than his own.

13

Jeremiah's Legacy

It might be supposed that a ministry so closely involved with the events of the prophet's own time could have few lasting effects, even though his interpretation of those tragic events was "laid forever on Judah's conscience." However, one permanent result is very clear: Judah never again played with idolatry or turned to her Gentile neighbors for models of worship and religious conduct.

In truth, Judah learned that lesson almost too well. Her genuine distinctiveness in religion hardened into a proud exclusiveness. While that helped to preserve her from absorption into Greek and Roman paganism, it also cut her off for centuries from the mainstream of human culture and development. In a similar way, Jeremiah's emphasis upon the divine requirements of the covenant later hardened into a legalism that exalted external, *measurable* standards of right and wrong, bound burdens on people's backs that they were unable to bear, bred intolerance of the weak and sinful, and tended to encourage self-righteousness — the worst product of religious zeal.

Thus post-exilic Judaism learned Jeremiah's lessons but

shared little of the profound understanding of God and personal devotion to him that gave those lessons meaning. As for Jeremiah's specific predictions, many went unfulfilled. There was no triumphant, exulting procession of returning exiles. There was no glorious reunion of Israel and Judah in the prosperous, singing life of city and countryside that Jeremiah had so lyrically described. And no "genuine Zedekiah" arose, no "shoot from David's stem" to reign as king and execute justice in the land. Yet the people of Judah did return to the land of their fathers. A remnant of faithful souls (the "Hasidim" or "pious ones") struggled to preserve the more spiritual insights at the heart of Judaism. And eventually the Messiah came with righteousness, grace, and a kingdom beyond anything even Jeremiah could foresee.

What, then, remains *today* of Jeremiah's memory, ministry, and martyrdom?

Social Righteousness

It is sometimes assumed that Jeremiah made no original contribution to the prophets' theme of social righteousness, that he simply repeated their denunciations but was chiefly concerned with Judah's religious infidelities. This is less than just. Certainly Jeremiah denounced the treachery and avarice of merchants, decried the injustice of the courts (5:26-29) as Amos had done, and deplored the low tone of society. He pleaded for fair treatment of the widow and the fatherless, the alien and the innocent, as Isaiah did, and condemned stealing, murder, adultery, greed, perjury, oppression, and violence — a comprehensive catalogue — with all the forthrightness of earlier prophets (7:5-11; 6:6-7, 13).

More positively, in words that might have been uttered by Isaiah, Jeremiah spoke of a king who would establish righteousness in the state. And he enunciated very clearly the moral conditions of true worship in the Lord's house: "Execute justice one with another, . . . do not oppress the alien, the fatherless or the widow, or shed innocent blood. . . . Has this house . . . become a den of robbers in your eyes?" (see 7:4-11).

Even on these themes, Jeremiah was no mere echo. Who could forget the blaze of anger with which he castigated the treachery of those who, at the height of the siege, solemnly swore to release their slaves, and then during a lull in the battle reasserted their slave-owning rights? Jeremiah saw this as typical of Judah's covenant-breaking faithlessness, but the human betrayal, the sheer cruelty of such conduct lent heat to his indignation. Or what could be more daring as social protest than Jeremiah's scornful public comparison of King Jehoiakim's ostentatious extravagance (at the price of forced labor) with the simpler, more just life-style of his godly father? So to expose the "dishonest gain, . . . oppression and violence" (22:17) of the king and prophesy for him "the burial of an ass" (22:19) was to challenge social inequality in high places at tremendous personal risk.

But if Jeremiah brought passionate conviction to ideas he shared with earlier prophets, he also added certain emphases of his own:

(i) Purity: Amos had condemned immoral rites at the hill shrines as a gross misrepresentation of the character of Israel's God. Jeremiah condemned them also, but more as a defilement and corruption of society itself. Jeremiah's lurid expressions make it clear that, at least in his earlier years, he was addressing a promiscuous, libertine society which "did not accept discipline" (7:28) and "polluted the land with . . . vile harlotry" (3:2).

That Jeremiah could use the language of adulterous infidelity to describe *also* Judah's unfaithfulness to God tends to obscure the occasions when he was referring to literal and lustful sexual immorality: "O Jerusalem, wash your heart from your wickedness" (4:14); "They were well-fed lusty stallions, each neighing for his neighbor's wife" (5:8); "I have seen your abominations, your adulteries and neighings, your lewd harlotries, on the hills in the field. Woe to you, O Jerusalem! How long will it be before you are made clean?" (13:27).

So we read of "orgies on the mountains" (3:23); people "not at all ashamed" who "did not know how to blush" (6:15); people who "refused to take correction," who "have made their faces harder than rock" (5:3). Such descriptions might be thought to apply rather to decadent Rome centuries later, but Jeremiah felt that the moral atmosphere of his own time among God's own people was polluted, licentious, and shameless. And he was conscious of all the consequent cost to family life, marital stability, women's dignity, and children's happiness.

(ii) Integrity: Again, other prophets had condemned the lack of honor in human relationships, the lack of truth in speech, and the lack of integrity in personal character. But Jeremiah placed quite exceptional emphasis on this feature of his society. There are frequent references to "lies," "falsehood," and "deceit" in the book of Jeremiah; these words occur at least sixty times. The prophet deplored the lack of even one just and honest citizen of Jerusalem (5:1); "truth has perished," he lamented (7:28), anticipating Isaiah's assertion that "truth has fallen in the public squares" (Isa. 59:14). He saw dishonesty and falseness infecting business, civic life, and religion itself.

Traders' houses are "full of treachery; therefore they have become great and rich" (5:27). Jeremiah finds himself amid "a company of treacherous men" who "bend their tongue like a bow," distorting speech and meaning (9:3). "Falsehood and not truth has grown strong in the land" (v. 3, RSV; the NIV has "it is not by truth that they triumph in the land," with the marginal gloss "they are not valiant for truth"). So they heap "deceit upon deceit" (9:6). "Let every one beware of his neighbor," Jeremiah warns, "and put no trust in any brother; for *every* brother is a supplanter [a Jacob]. . . . Every one deceives his neighbor, and no one speaks the truth; they have *taught* their tongue to speak lies [by careful plotting, by practice, and by sharpened cunning]. . . . With his mouth each speaks peaceably to his neighbor, but in his heart he plans an ambush for him" (9:4-9, emphasis mine). The situation is not unknown today.

Even in religion men swear falsely, complains Jeremiah. They use the name of God only to deceive; prophets, priests, and people deal falsely, and lies are told in God's name by prophets who have lost all sense of the sacredness of truth (5:12, 30, 31; 6:13; 8:10; 23:25-32). As a result, the people trust in deceptive slogans ("the temple of the Lord," 7:4) and actually prefer what is false ("they hold fast to deceit," 8:5); they "trust in a lie" (28:15), hating the truth (see also 3:10; 7:8).

Jeremiah is equally aware of the most dangerous falsehood of all, the lie within the soul. "The heart is deceitful above all things" (17:9); "How long shall there be lies in the heart of the prophets?" (23:26); "Do not deceive *yourselves*" (37:9, emphasis mine). This is the deepest corruption of the individual and of society: loss of the power to discern truth from falsehood, or to care which is which. For Jeremiah, there could be no dealing with "the true God" (10:10) except on the basis of frankness, integrity, and realism. A society built upon self-deception and falsehood to others alienated itself from God and prepared the way for its own downfall — "What will you do when the end comes?" (5:31).

(iii) Society's Foundations: The third emphasis which is not Jeremiah's alone but which is especially prominent in his thought is that social welfare and security *depend upon* a right relationship with God. He believed that the character of a society is determined by its fulfillment or betrayal of the divine

covenant, not by superficial religious observances; a society's direction and discipline, its moral tone, feeling, values, and loyalties spring from an understanding of life and its purpose that is basically religious.

A community without religion soon lacks effective moral leadership, is devoid of any united moral outlook or compelling social obligations. It can generate no cohesive social drive and find no firm basis for civic order and restraint such as a simple, clear creed and a protective moral code can provide. A civic "order" based only on the whim of a ruling class, on temporary agreement among the majority to bully dissidents into conformity, or on the assertion of unlimited human "rights" while mutual responsibility is denied *must,* quite inevitably, decay into disorder. For there is nothing in education, culture, or individual self-interest to eradicate — or even to restrain — impulses of greed, envy, self-assertion, revenge, pride, and violence, which continually threaten social unity. Inspiring motives, gentling sensitivity, restraining fear, and moral responsibility all spring only from genuine religious conviction, reverence, and experience.

This is the understanding of society that finds expression in Jeremiah's words — "a man's life is not his own; it is not for man to direct his steps" (10:23, NIV) — and lies behind his insistence that only in careful observance of her covenant with the God who "practice[s] steadfast love, justice, and righteousness in the earth" would Judah ever find security (9:24). And the same crucial insight into the foundations of social welfare prompts his tracing of Judah's malaise to a fundamental skepticism: "The fear of [the Lord] is not in you" (2:19); "They have spoken falsely of the Lord, and have said, 'He will do nothing; no evil will come upon us. . . . The prophets will become wind; the word is not in them'" (5:12-13; see also 14:13; 23:17). Under outward pressure and inward corruption, such a society could only collapse.

It is scarcely fair to say that a man who could write in this way made no significant contribution to the Bible's social teaching, even if we admit that the broad outline of his message was one he shared with earlier prophetic teachers.

Individual and Corporate Religion

But the fundamental change that Jeremiah brought about in the very concept of religion was very much his own. As we have seen (in the commentary on 31:27-30), from earliest times in Israel religion had been a function of communal life. The group (family, clan, tribe, nation) in which the growing individual found himself or herself possessed inherited beliefs, myths, rituals, customs, taboos, and obligations that he or she in turn shared as a member of the community. The experience of religion as joy, fear, duty, and worship was mediated to him or her through the group, controlled and disciplined by the group, and expressed through corporate activities.

Thus, to be excluded from one's tribe — by capture, rebellion, slavery, or ban — was to be excluded from the rites, reassurance, protection, and experiences of the tribe's religion. This explains David's lament: "They have driven me out this day, that I should have no share in the heritage of the Lord, saying, 'Go, serve other gods'" (1 Sam. 26:19). Even lonely and persecuted pioneers in religious thought and action, like Samuel, Elijah, and Amos, while they rose above the average level of communal religion, remained a product and a part of the community that shaped them.

But Jeremiah found himself initially self-excluded from the religious community by his critical attitude toward the syncretist version of the Israelite tradition that confronted him, first at Anathoth and later at Jerusalem. Later, he became even more isolated from the religious community because of its total rejection of him. A deep alienation from priests, prophets, and devotees of current religion found sharpening expression in Jeremiah's increasing criticism of sacrifices, the temple, the sacred book, the holy city, and the "inspired" leaders of the current cultus. He could hardly have been more thoroughly excluded from the corporate religious institution of his people.

And yet he found he was not without God. In no sense was he excluded from religious experience or released from religious obligation — both were immeasurably intensified by his isolation. In his solitude he pondered the original roots of Israel's faith and nationhood, the character of God, and his own relationship with God. He believed himself called, irrevocably, to the service of the God whom Israel herself had so largely forsaken. No ill treatment from the community's religious authorities released him from that allegiance. He began, though reluctantly, to serve the God of the community that excluded him, and found God with him.

In isolation he developed that "daring familiarity" which prompted prayers, protests, complaints, resentments, and arguments addressed directly to God himself. In loneliness, often in prison, brooding upon his paradoxical experience, Jeremiah turned of necessity inward and Godward, and found God accessible and responsive. Repeatedly laying bare his own soul and pleading for healing for his own heart, he also brought before God the sins, follies, and perils of his people, an "unofficial" priest now, but more closely identified with Judah and pleading for her more passionately than ever.

And so Jeremiah came to stand "in the council of the Lord" (23:18, 22), to learn God's ways, understand his mind, comprehend his purposes, and experience his favor and help to a degree that no community could hope to match or could hope to communicate to him. The cost of that individual discovery was high, but its reward, in knowledge of God and fellowship with him, was immeasurable. In this way, as one commentator has pointed out, "It is to the torture of Jeremiah's soul that man owes one of his most glorious possessions, the birthright of individual fellowship with God."

What is equally remarkable, however, is that in finding this new truth, Jeremiah did not lose the older truth of solidarity in shared faith, tradition, and experience. The new covenant of divine law written on the individual heart, where once sin had been so deeply engraved (17:1), was still to be established with *Israel and Judah,* the renewed "people of God" (recall the commentary on 31:31-34, pp. 128-30).

But now the individual's experience of God was the ground of membership in that community, instead of membership in the community being the ground of religious status, faith, and meaning for the individual. Although the individual no longer found God only through the community, still a religious community emerged and was renewed from generation to generation as the faith inherited became "alive" and "operative" in new individuals. Still mediated corporately (and this holds true today as well) were the initiating impulse toward religious experience, the witness to its truth, the forms of worship, and the norms of conduct that express and support individual faith. By heritage and priestly training, Jeremiah was well aware of the importance of shared worship, custom, and discipline if religious life was to be strong, balanced, socially effective, and cohesive.

Nevertheless, it was the intensely individual, person-to-person experience of God that was Jeremiah's epoch-making discovery. It was not merely emotional, ecstatic, or mystical; it was a strong, undergirding, and fruitful relationship that engendered (as we have seen) profound thought, a social conscience, a high personal ethic, and a comprehensive view of the divine purpose. Moreover, the new individualized conception of religion had far-reaching consequences.

Implications

(i) Individuality: Inevitably, Jeremiah's new emphasis implied a wholly new assessment of the importance of the individual, his or her opportunities, responsibilities, powers, and significance. Jeremiah's whole ministry reminds us that all history is God's field of activity: his canvas is as wide as the known world, and his themes the actions and policies of nations. Yet always God's agents are individuals — prophets, priests, kings, captains, "my servant, Nebuchadrezzar" — all playing their individual roles but achieving God's purposes. So individuals who know God, each for himself or herself, unite as "the people of God" and become a world force for good.

The individual is never submerged. The individual's private response to God, inward acceptance of divine law as self-discipline, personal covenant with God, and commitment to the things God "delights in" — all are crucial. God chooses his individual, sets him or her a task in the circumstances appointed for him or her, and receives absolute obedience. No obligation to others rivals this obligation to God; no comparison with others' experience or duties modifies the personal obligation: "Others may, but you may not; others need not, but you must." And God has no need to justify his demands or his ways to his servants. God will fortify ("as brass"), sustain, and in the end vindicate; for the individual who knows God, that is enough.

Such individuality of religious experience fosters great variety of character, insight, vocation, devotion, sensitivity, attainment, and testimony. The classic expression of this variety is the Hebrew psalter, and it is significant that many of the most personal psalms (Pss. 23, 51, 73, and 139 are but examples) could not have been written before Jeremiah found religion to be intensely personal. Spiritual unity among those who "know God" — a unity of mutual respect, sympathy, and shared purposes and worship — stands high among religious values; but since Jeremiah, unity can never descend again to the stereotyped, impersonal uniformity of tribal religion.

(ii) Immortality: At a more distant remove, Jeremiah's assertion of individual, personal relationship with God made necessary a revision of Judaist thought of the afterlife. Sheol, the abode of the dead, represented a mere shadow-play of the earthly community, in which all human individuality, all personal variety and character, had been left behind: "In death there is no remembrance of thee; in Sheol who can give thee praise?" (Ps. 6:5); "Dost thou work wonders for the dead? Do the shades rise up to praise thee? Is thy steadfast love declared in the grave, or thy faithfulness in Abaddon? Are thy wonders known in the darkness, or thy saving help in the land of forgetfulness?" (Ps. 88:10-12); "There is no work or thought or knowledge or wisdom in Sheol, to which you are going" (Eccl. 9:10); "Those who go down to the pit cannot hope for thy faithfulness" (Isa. 38:18). As Jeremiah might say, in Sheol there is no opportunity for life's greatest prize, "the knowledge of God" (see also Ps. 30:9; Ps. 115:17).

But with the new appreciation of the worth of the individual in God's sight came a more truly human conception of life after death, with some continuance of personal character and moral (and social) distinctions in the underworld; eventually came the imported notion of a semi-physical resurrection to complete the whole person. With this arose a new argument for immortality: that God would not abandon to dust and darkness those whom he had admitted to fellowship and to covenanted relationship with him. "Surely goodness and mercy shall follow me all the days of my life; and I shall dwell in the house of the Lord for ever" (Ps. 23:6); "I am continually with thee; thou dost hold my right hand. Thou dost guide me with thy counsel, and afterward thou wilt receive me to glory" (Ps.

73:23-24); "O Lord, thou hast searched me and known me! . . . Whither shall I go from thy Spirit? . . . If I ascend to heaven, thou art there! If I make my bed in Sheol, thou art there!" (Ps. 139:1, 7-8).

It is indeed a long, long step from Jeremiah to Jesus, yet it was Jeremiah's "discovery" of individual knowledge of God and relationship with him that prepared the way for Jesus' declaration: "That the dead are raised, even Moses showed, in the passage about the bush, where he calls the Lord the God of Abraham and the God of Isaac and the God of Jacob. Now he is not God of the dead, but of the living; for all live to him" (Luke 20:37-38).

(iii) Universality: Equally distant and indirect is a further consequence of Jeremiah's thought. As we noted earlier (see the commentary on 31:31-34, pp. 128-30), a divine covenant based upon individual knowledge of God and personal obedience to his will must eventually be seen to be inter-racial. Hitherto, the foundation of Judah's election had lain in God's choice of Abraham and the blood relationship with him thought to be expressed in circumcision. The family-nation was the covenantal unit. But with Jeremiah the basis of the covenant becomes God's gracious initiative responded to by individual faith and obedience, and that response is possible for Ebed-melech the Ethiopian (39:16-18) and for nations from the ends of the earth, who will turn from idols to know the power and might and name of the Lord (16:19-21).

In the end, this insight was to destroy the exclusive "Jewish privilege" with God, as Paul felt and feared that it would. The unresolved tension in his mind can still be felt in those passages in which he wrestles with the precious truth of Israel's election and the necessary redefinition of Israel if all having faith in Jesus are inheritors of Abraham's faith and favor (Rom. 2:28-29; 4:16; chaps. 9-11). Here, too, the distance from Jeremiah's thought is great, but a line runs inexorably from

Jeremiah to James' quotation ("I will rebuild the dwelling of David . . . , that the rest of men may seek the Lord, and all the Gentiles who are called by my name"; Acts 15:16-17), to Peter's declaration ("Truly I perceive that God shows no partiality, but in every nation any one who fears him and does what is right is acceptable to him"; Acts 10:35), to John's assertion ("The Father has sent his Son as the Savior of *the world*"; 1 John 4:14, emphasis mine).

(iv) Jeremiah's Gospel: There is no need to doubt the awe, fear, and contagious ecstasy of great religious occasions when clan, tribe, or nation celebrated great festivals or merciful deliverances. But there can be no question that Jeremiah's insight opened new depths of fervor, anguish, and joy in religious experience. A more emotional, more "human" tone marks the new prophetic conception of "love" for God, which is mentioned eleven times in the book of Deuteronomy (and probably not earlier). In that ancient world it would be a novel idea. The individual's intimate knowledge of God became life's highest value, and personal — rather than tribal — forgiveness, reassurance, and promise became so much more important as they came "home" to the individual heart. At the same time, they came to provide a moral motivation that reached new heights of aspiration and loyalty as individuals "laid hold of God," their "exceeding great reward."

This is the new quality of religion that informs the psalter, where a wholly new vocabulary of love, longing, joy, penitence, praise, exultation, thanksgiving, testimony, and delight in God (contrasted, say, with the vocabulary of the book of Leviticus) reveals to what new heights of religious experience Jeremiah's individual covenanting with God has lifted Judaism. Henceforth in Jewish thought the wider issues of national destiny yield place, to no small extent, to issues of individual salvation, to means of personal redemption, to problems of individual suffering (as in the book of Job), to questions of personal immortality, to the mission of proselytization (as in the book of Jonah), to the quest for individual righteousness (the Pharisees) and personal sanctification (the Essenes).

In ways thus revolutionary and far-reaching, more important than the fulfillment of detailed predictions, the whole significance of Jeremiah's life and ministry is vindicated before history. Such a legacy to humankind gives immense spiritual meaning and force to his own final utterance:

"[They] shall know whose word will stand, mine or theirs" (44:28).

The Commentary

in biblical order
(See also Index of Scripture References)

Index of Names and Subjects

Index of Scripture References